A Literary
Tea Party

A Literary Tea Party

Blends and Treats for Alice, Bilbo, Dorothy, Jo, and Book Lovers Everywhere

Alison Walsh
Introduction by Sara Letourneau

Skyhorse Publishing

Skyhorse Publishing books may be purchased in bulk at special discounts for sales promotion, corporate gifts, fund-raising, or educational purposes. Special editions can also be created to specifications. For details, contact the Special Sales Department, Skyhorse Publishing, 307 West 36th Street, 11th Floor, New York, NY 10018 or info@ skyhorsepublishing.com.

Skyhorse® and Skyhorse Publishing® are registered trademarks of Skyhorse Publishing, Inc.®, a Delaware corporation.

Visit our website at www.skyhorsepublishing.com.

10 9 8 7 6

Library of Congress Cataloging-in-Publication Data is available on file.

Cover design by Abigail Gehring
Cover illustration credit: iStockphoto
Photographs by Alison Walsh

Print ISBN: 978-1-5107-2910-0
Ebook ISBN: 978-1-5107-2912-4

Printed in China

For the Mister, my always eager taste tester,

and

for the Little Mister, who was with me every step of the way

table of contents

introduction

by Sara Letourneau

Have you ever wondered why food and drink appear so often in great stories? Or why we frequently find characters sharing meals with family, friends, and the occasional stranger? If your first guess is, "Because the author wants to make us readers hungry," well, no one would fault you (or your taste buds) for thinking that way. But here's the truth:

If literature is meant to reflect life, then why not use food, a part of our everyday lives, to make that reflection truly believable?

Think about it for a moment. Food can provide insights into our favorite heroes, heroines, and mischief-makers. (Remember when Aunt Polly caught Tom Sawyer sneaking jam from the pantry?) It can evoke smells and flavors that bring a setting to life and stir up emotions that deepen a reader's connection in the story. Some stories such as Laura Ingalls Wilders's Little House series and Louisa May Alcott's *Little Women* even feature cooks and bakers as characters.

And who can forget when the White Witch offered Edmund hot chocolate and Turkish delight in *The Lion, the Witch, and the Wardrobe*? Or when Harry Potter and his classmates sat down for their first banquet at Hogwarts? Or when Alice stumbles upon the Mad Hatter and the March Hare's tea party? The sharing of food is a natural opportunity for characters to interact and demonstrate their relationships, from family and friendships to travelers on the same road and villains tempting their prey.

Indeed, food and drink have played a deliciously meaningful role in literature. It's something I've relished as a lifelong lover of reading. Thanks to timeless stories like J.R.R. Tolkien's *The Hobbit* and Geoffrey Chaucer's *Canterbury Tales*, and more recent books like Laura Esquivel's *Like Water for Chocolate* and Suzanne Collins's *The Hunger Games*, I've lost count of how many times I've smacked my lips over the proffered dishes or marveled over the conversations, arguments, and awkward silences that follow. Even my nighttime reading involves nourishment; I have to have a mug of freshly brewed tea beside me, or else the ritual feels incomplete.

And on top of all this, I've wondered now and then how much fun—and how challenging—it might be to recreate some of the foods I've read about. It's not a far-fetched idea, since I also enjoy cooking and baking. But I've always felt more comfortable following recipes than inventing my own. My imagination could play forever when it comes to writing stories, poems, and blog articles, but in the kitchen it usually grinds to a halt.

1

Thankfully, that's where Alison Walsh comes in. An avid reader herself, Alison has taken her enthusiasm to a whole other level, beginning with her food blog *Alison's Wonderland Recipes*. I discovered the site in 2015, and I was immediately drawn in by the charm and excitement she exuded in bringing much-loved dishes from fiction to edible reality. The variety of foods, easy-to-follow instructions, cleanly presented photographs—all of it enticed me to return week after week to try the recipes at home. It also helped that Alison and I shared similar reading tastes and a passion for tea. And now, to say that I'm thrilled about Alison's latest culinary and literary achievement would be an understatement.

A Literary Tea Party puts a whimsical "stir" on literary cookbooks. It doesn't just serve recipes inspired by foods from classic literature. It also presents carefully crafted and specifically selected dishes that are ideal for—what else?—teatime. From scones, breads, and finger-food savories to cookies and other bite-size sweets, this is an elegant and heartwarming tribute to the stories and characters that have stayed with us. You'll also find recipes for unique homemade tea blends that will bring additional warmth, fragrance, and complexity to the meal. And if you're not a tea lover, then maybe the hot cocoa, punches, and other beverages will tickle your taste buds.

So make yourself a cup of tea and see which recipes catch your eye. Do any come from books you read as a child and still rank among your all-time favorites? Try those foods first to savor the nostalgia and remember why you loved the book in the first place. And who knows? Maybe Alison's work will inspire you to plan a themed tea party, one with decorations, attire, and, of course, a menu drawing from some of the most memorable stories ever written.

a letter from the author

Dear Reader,

If you told me four years ago that I'd publish a cookbook—any cookbook, ever—I wouldn't have believed you. At the time, my love of cooking was just beginning to sprout, and my culinary experience was limited to meals for one and the occasional dinner party with friends. When I started my little fledgling food blog, *Alison's Wonderland Recipes*, all I knew was that I wanted to combine my new love of food with my lifelong love of reading.

When Skyhorse emailed me about writing a cookbook, I had been blogging for three years. My skill level was much higher than when I started, but I still had a lot to learn. I could concoct a soup and grill a mean steak, but I had no idea how to develop my own bread or cake recipes. Still, I knew one thing: there was *no way* I was going to say no!

So I went for it. I didn't know the science behind things like baking and candymaking, but I learned. I compared reliable recipes and noted shared variables. I watched more YouTube videos about making Turkish delight than anyone ever should. I made it my goal to add one completely original recipe to my blog every month to challenge myself to learn new skills.

My point in saying all of this is that I didn't embark on this project because I felt ready; instead, I became ready by doing it. In the process, not only did I find that I was more capable than I thought, my efforts also jumpstarted my learning like nothing before. I'm a much better chef, blogger, recipe developer, writer, and time manager than I would be now if I'd passed up this amazing opportunity.

If there's anything you're afraid you're not good enough for, don't let fear make your choices. We all have doubts about ourselves, but life has a way of helping us grow past those doubts, if we only let it.

So if you have a chance to spread your wings, don't pass it up. You have more to give than you realize, and the lessons you'll learn will be priceless.

Alison
Creator of *Alison's Wonderland Recipes*,
wonderlandrecipes.com

tips, tricks, and substitutions

Every chef needs a few good shortcuts up their sleeve to save the day when they're short on time or don't have a special ingredient. Here are my favorite kitchen tips and tricks:

DIY Double Boiler. If you don't have a double boiler, just place a regular ceramic bowl over a saucepan of boiling water. Make sure the water level is low enough so that the bottom of the bowl doesn't touch the top of the water.

Quick Buttermilk Substitute. Mix 1 cup milk with 1 tablespoon lemon juice and allow to sit for 5 minutes.

Room Temperature Eggs. If a recipe calls for room temperature eggs and you forgot to let them sit out, submerge the eggs in very warm water for 10 minutes, then use as per normal.

Instant Softened Butter. Sometimes I don't have the time to soften butter or my winter kitchen isn't warm enough for it to soften when left to sit out. To instantly soften butter, place it between two sheets of wax paper and roll it to about ¼-inch thickness with a rolling pin. Quickly peel off the paper and use as per normal.

Liquid vs. Gel Food Coloring. Some of the recipes in this book call for gel food coloring, while some call for standard liquid coloring. Gel is more condensed and therefore introduces less water into the recipe, while achieving more intense color. I've specified the use of gel coloring in recipes where it's recommended, but if it's an emergency and you need to substitute it, the conversion is easy: use 2–3 drops of liquid for every drop of gel.

Edible Flowers. Some of the recipes in this book call for edible flowers. Pansies are a common choice in edible flower recipes, as are blossoms from strawberry, apple, and citrus plants. The Internet is a great way to find additional safe alternatives. Always use clean blossoms that you know are free of pesticides and chemicals, and be aware that although a plant may have edible blossoms, this does not make all parts of the plant safe to eat.

Quick Dough Cleanup. Many cookie recipes call for flouring a surface (usually a countertop) and rolling out dough. If quick cleanup is a priority, roll out your dough on a large floured cutting board, which can be quickly rinsed off and/or thrown in the dishwasher when finished.

Sticky Measuring Spoons. Accurately measuring sticky liquid ingredients like honey and syrup can be a pain—some of it always manages to stick to the spoon! For some recipes, you can avoid this by coating the spoon in a thin layer of cooking spray before adding in your ingredient, as long as fats such as butter or eggs will be added in the same step or have already been added. For example, if you are making muffins that call for honey, you can spray the spoon if you're adding your fats in the same step or if they've already been mixed in. For recipes that are very finicky about the addition of fats (such as meringues), do not use this trick as it can add too much fat to the recipe.

Swapping Salted and Unsalted Butter. Some recipes call for unsalted butter yet still include salt in the list of ingredients. This is to allow for exact measurements and a more consistent result. However, if you are in a bind and don't have the right butter, don't panic. There is approximately ¼ tsp salt in every ½ cup salted butter, so use this ratio to adjust your recipe in an emergency. Although it's not recommended for regular use, it shouldn't make a huge difference. This cannot be done for recipes that call for no salt at all, such as some pie crusts.

themed tea party ideas

Planning a party can be overwhelming, but a theme helps narrow down your options to make the whole experience more manageable. With that in mind, I've provided some tea party themes below with suggested recipes and tea blends. Some are book-specific (such as Aslan's Feast), while other themes are more general and draw their inspiration from multiple books (like the Children's Tea Party). Many work well in multiple scenarios, so try them out at birthdays, baby showers, and even book club meetings!

Alice's Mad Tea Party

Bread and Butterflies *Through the Looking Glass* (p. 19)

Panther's Pasties *Alice's Adventures in Wonderland* (p. 37)

Stuffed Button Mushrooms *Alice's Adventures in Wonderland* (p. 46)

Queen of Hearts' Painted Rose Cupcakes *Alice's Adventures in Wonderland* (p. 107)

Drink Me Tea *Alice's Adventures in Wonderland* (p. 121)

Aslan's Feast

Apple of Life Bites *The Chronicles of Narnia* (p. 13)

Mr. and Mrs. Beaver's Ham Sandwiches *The Chronicles of Narnia* (p. 35)

Scotch Eggs *The Chronicles of Narnia* (p. 43)

Lemon Turkish Delight *The Chronicles of Narnia* (p. 99)

White Witch Hot Chocolate *The Chronicles of Narnia* (p. 139)

Tea with Tumnus *The Chronicles of Narnia* (p. 126)

An Autumnal Tea Party

Haycorns for Piglet *Winnie-the-Pooh* (p. 31)

Deeper 'n Ever Turnip 'n Tater 'n Beetroot Pie *Redwall* (p. 23)

Beorn's Honey Nut Banana Bread *The Hobbit* (p. 53)

Candied Nuts with Meadowcream *Redwall* (p. 77)

Autumn Harvest Cider *Redwall* (p. 131)

Abbot's Chocolate Hazelnut Tea *Redwall* (p. 119)

Children's Tea Party

Cracked China Deviled Eggs *The Wonderful Wizard of Oz* (p. 21)

Bread and Butterflies *Through the Looking Glass* (p. 19)

Toasted Cheese Buns *Treasure Island* (p. 65)

Fairy Dust Star Cookies *Peter Pan* (p. 89)

Eeyore's Birthday Cake *Winnie-the-Pooh* (p. 87)

Raspberry Cordial *Anne of Green Gables* (p. 137)

Arrietty's Cherry Tree Tea *The Borrowers* (p. 119)

Murder Most Delicious: A Detective Tea Party

Blood Orange Scones *Sherlock Holmes* (p. 57)

Miss Marple's "Pocket Full of Rye" Tea Sandwiches *Agatha Christie* (p. 32)

Dark Chocolate Earl Grey Lavender Truffles *Sherlock Holmes* (p. 79)

Delicious Death Chocolate Cake *Agatha Christie* (p. 81)

London Fog Lattes *Sherlock Holmes* (p. 135)

Poirot's Chocolate Mate Tea *Agatha Christie* (p. 124)

Teatime Garden Party

Blackberry Lemon Sweet Rolls *A Little Princess* (p. 55)

Poetical Egg Salad Sandwiches *Anne of Green Gables* (p. 41)

Badger's Set Salad Bites *The Borrowers* (p. 15)

Candied Flower Cookies *The Secret Garden* (p. 71)

Lavender Lemon Eclairs *The Secret Garden* (p. 97)

Raspberry Cordial *Anne of Green Gables* (p. 137)

Miss Mary's Garden Blend *The Secret Garden* (p. 123)

A Valentine's Day Tea Party

Star-Crossed Focaccia with Parmesan Chive Butter *Romeo and Juliet* (p. 63)

Phantom's Savory Apple Rose Tartlets *The Phantom of the Opera* (p. 39)

Romeo's Sighs and Juliet's Kisses *Romeo and Juliet* (p. 109)

Arrietty's Mini Cherry Cakes *The Borrowers* (p. 69)

Lovers' Tea *Romeo and Juliet* (p. 123)

savories

In literature, savory foods are often used to give us insight into characters' personalities. In Agatha Christie's Hercule Poirot mysteries, the fastidious, orderly detective breakfasts on the same thing every day: two perfectly identical eggs and a piece of toast cut into perfect squares. In *A Little Princess*, the imaginative Sara Crewe copes with hunger by dreaming up a grand, exotic feast to sustain herself.

By observing the meals of characters, the reader is able to bond with them over one of the most fundamental shared human experiences: food. And when we cook their foods in our own kitchens, we connect with them even more. We bridge the gap between fiction and reality, making real that which was previously just fantasy.

As we prepare food we've read about in books and slide it out steaming from our ovens, characters become more than just words on a page—their world becomes a reality in our own homes.

apple of life bites

from *The Magician's Nephew* by C. S. Lewis

Makes 8 apple disks

"He knew which was the right tree at once, partly because it stood in the very center and partly because the great silvery apples with which it was loaded shone so and cast a light of their own down on the shadowy places where the sunlight did not reach."

This easy snack brings together sweet-tart apples, salty bacon, savory pecans, and smooth crème de brie for a fun twist on apple slices.

INGREDIENTS

4 slices bacon
1 Granny Smith apple
½ cup (approximately
  2.5 oz) crème de Brie
3 tsp pecan chips,
  toasted if desired

INSTRUCTIONS

1 Fry the bacon and allow it to drain on a plate lined with a paper towel. Chop the bacon into bits.

2 Core and slice the apple into ¼-inch-thick disks.

3 Spread each disk with 1 tablespoon of crème de Brie. Sprinkle on the pecan chips and chopped bacon.

Serve at a magnificent Narnian feast!

Tea pairing

Tea with Tumnus,
p. 126

badger's set salad bites

from *The Borrowers* by Mary Norton

Makes 15 salad bites

*"They had hips and haws and blackberries and sloes and wild strawberries . . .
Think of a salad made of those tender shoots of young hawthorn . . .
with sorrel and dandelion . . . Homily was a good cook remember."*

These fresh and fruity salad bites offer a true balance of flavors: sweet berries, salty seeds, slightly earthy greens, and a bit of bite from the strawberry balsamic vinegar.

INGREDIENTS

15 dandelion greens*
8 small strawberries
30 blueberries
  (approximately ½ cup)
Edible flowers**
3 Tbsp salted
  sunflower seeds
Strawberry balsamic
  vinegar***

Special Tools
15 toothpicks

Tea pairing

Arrietty's Cherry
Tree Tea, p. 119

INSTRUCTIONS

1   Rinse and dry your greens and berries. Check your greens for any that have bristly hairs on their spines. Store-bought dandelion greens usually come in bundles, so only choose greens with smooth spines from the bundle.

2   Trim your greens into 4-inch long strips and cut the strawberries into wedges.

3   To assemble, insert a toothpick through one end of a dandelion green and slide the green to the bottom of the toothpick. Slide a strawberry wedge and a blueberry width-wise onto the toothpick. Then slide on another strawberry wedge and blueberry. Insert the toothpick through the other end of the dandelion green. Depending on the flowers you use, they may be sturdy enough to be inserted onto the toothpick. Delicate blossoms can be tucked in beside the berries. To finish, sprinkle on some sunflower seeds.

4   Repeat Step 3 with the remaining salad components.

5   Sprinkle some strawberry vinegar onto the salad bites.

Serve while visiting your favorite Borrower at their badger's set home!

* Dandelion greens can be found at most major grocery stores when they are in season, which is January through May.

** The salad bites pictured feature strawberry blossoms. Be sure to use flowers that are clean and free of pesticides and chemicals.

*** To make your own strawberry balsamic vinegar, coarsely chop 3 large or 5 medium strawberries and place them in a mason jar. Completely submerge the strawberries in white balsamic vinegar. Seal the container and leave it to sit overnight at room temperature. After that, strain out and discard the strawberries. Store the strawberry balsamic vinegar in a sealed mason jar in the refrigerator.

big apple hand pies

from *James and the Giant Peach* by Roald Dahl

Makes 12 hand pies

"And suddenly—everyone who had come over on the peach was a hero! They were all escorted to the steps of City Hall, where the Mayor of New York made a speech of welcome."

These savory hand pies are filled with melted Gouda and apple slices seasoned with thyme. Named for James's final destination—the Big Apple—their buttery, flaky crust topped with a dash of salt brings it all together into a tiny package filled with big flavor.

INGREDIENTS

¼ small Gala apple
1 tsp thyme*
1–2 oz Gouda cheese
2 sheets premade
   pie dough
1 egg, lightly beaten
½ tsp kosher salt

SPECIAL TOOLS

3-inch apple-shaped
   cookie cutter

Tea pairing

Summery Peach Tea,
p. 126

* You can also substitute ½ tsp cinnamon for 1 tsp thyme if you'd like to emphasize the sweet flavors over the savory.

INSTRUCTIONS

1 Preheat oven to 350°F. Line a baking sheet with parchment paper and set aside.

2 Slice the apple quarter into 6 slices. Cut the slices in half width-wise.

3 Toss the apple pieces in a small bowl with thyme and set aside.

4 Cut the Gouda into 12 1¼-inch squares. Set aside.

5 On a lightly floured surface, unroll the first sheet of pie dough (keep the second sheet in the fridge until you're ready for it). Cut 12 apple shapes out of the dough and evenly space them on the prepared baking sheet.

6 Place an apple slice in the center of each piece of dough and place a Gouda square on top. Brush the edges of the dough with the beaten egg.

7 Unroll your second sheet of pie dough and cut out 12 more apple shapes. Place them on top of the first set of cutouts and crimp the edges with a fork.

8 Brush the tops of the hand pies with the beaten egg and prick each one 2–3 times with a fork. Sprinkle with kosher salt.

9 Bake for 17 minutes or until golden brown on top.

Serve warm after a long journey to New York City!

bread and butterflies

from *Through the Looking Glass* by Lewis Carroll

Makes 10 bite-size sandwiches

"Its wings are thin slices of Bread-and-butter, its body is a crust, and its head is a lump of sugar."

The key to a good cucumber sandwich is delicacy and quality ingredients. Things like slicing the cucumbers thin and splurging on fancy butter (such as Kerrygold) go a long way here!

INGREDIENTS

¼ cup softened butter
1 Tbsp snipped
  fresh chives
10 slices white bread*
1–2 mini cucumbers, cut
  into 20 thin disks
10 3-inch lengths
  fresh chives
10 small sprigs fresh dill**

Special Tools

2½-inch heart-shaped
  cookie cutter

Tea pairing

Drink Me Tea, p. 121

* Breads that come in wider loaves like oatmeal bread work well for this recipe, since it will be easier to cut two hearts from each slice.

** Use enough to put 4 tiny tufts of dill on each sandwich.

INSTRUCTIONS

1   In a small bowl, mix the butter with the snipped fresh chives and set aside.

2   Cut your bread into 20 hearts (you should get 2 hearts from each slice). Thinly spread the chive butter onto the hearts.

3   Cut 10 of your cucumber disks in half to make half-moon shapes. On 10 of your hearts, place 1 full disk near the bottom of each heart and a half-moon piece in each of the two curves near the top. It should look like the image below.

4   Place your remaining hearts on top, butter side down. Place a 3-inch length of chive down the center of each sandwich and 2 tufts of dill on each "wing."

Serve at a Mad Tea Party!

cracked china deviled eggs

from *The Wonderful Wizard of Oz* by L. Frank Baum

Makes 24 deviled eggs

"But whenever any of us are taken away our joints at once stiffen, and we can only stand straight and look pretty. . . our lives are much pleasanter here in our own country."
—The China Princess

I developed this recipe in honor of some of my favorite characters from *The Wonderful Wizard of Oz*: the little china people. I love how they all have courageous spirits, despite being so delicate. The milkmaid takes no nonsense from anybody, and the jester doesn't let a few cracks stop him from doing headstands!

INGREDIENTS

1 dozen eggs
Gel food coloring, various colors
1 cup mayonnaise
1½ Tbsp mustard
1 tsp parsley flakes
1 tsp chives
½ tsp salt

NOTE: When Easter rolls around, these eggs are a creative alternative to traditional dyed eggs. You can also use black dye to turn them into Halloween eggs.

INSTRUCTIONS

1 Place the eggs in the bottom of a large pot. Fill with cold water until the eggs are under 2 inches of water. Place on high heat. When the water comes to a boil, remove from heat and cover for 7 minutes. Drain and allow the eggs to cool.

2 Fill 6 large mugs about ⅔ full with cold water. Place the mugs on a baking sheet to avoid staining anything if there are spills. Put 3–4 drops gel food coloring in each mug and stir until completely dissolved.

3 When the eggs are cooled, gently crack each one in several places by tapping them against the counter and rotating as you tap. Try to create a lot of tiny cracks but not so many that the shell falls off.

4 Leaving the cracked shell in place, lower two eggs into each mug of food coloring. Put the mugs in the fridge for 7–12 hours.

5 Remove the eggs from the mugs and pat dry with a paper towel. Gently peel the shell from each egg, revealing the "cracked china" color effect.

6 Cut each egg in half lengthwise and set the yolk halves aside in a bowl. Set the white halves on a serving plate.

7 Mix the yolks with the mayonnaise, mustard, parsley flakes, chives, and salt. This can be done with a spoon for a coarse texture or with a hand mixer for a smooth texture. If using a spoon to mash the filling, make sure any chunks of yolk are small enough to allow for piping.

8 Spoon the filling into a piping bag fitted with a large round tip. Pipe about 1½ teaspoons of filling into each egg half.

Serve to the lively porcelain China People in Oz!

deeper 'n ever turnip 'n tater 'n beetroot pie

from *The Rogue Crew: A Tale of Redwall* by Brian Jacques

Makes one 9-inch pie

*"There ain't no better cook in all of Mossflower than Friar Wopple.
She makes pies an' soups, an' pasties . . . an' deeper 'n ever turnip 'n tater 'n
beetroot pie for the moles. Best food you ever tasted . . ."*
—Uggo

The ultimate root vegetable dish, this savory pie boasts buttery herbed crust and hearty diced vegetable filling with a flavor reminiscent of Thanksgiving stuffing. Like all the recipes eaten by the beasts of Redwall, it's naturally vegetarian . . .but I won't fault you if you add some diced chicken!

INGREDIENTS

Filling
1 cup chopped
    sweet onion
½ cup butternut squash,
    peeled and cubed
1 cup white turnip, peeled
    and cubed
1 cup parsnip, peeled
    and cubed
1 cup beets, peeled
    and cubed
1 cup carrots, peeled
    and cubed
1 cup chopped celery
1 cup sliced mushrooms
3 Tbsp olive oil
½ tsp salt
¼ tsp pepper

Binding Mix
4 red potatoes
2 cloves garlic, minced
½ tsp salt
1 Tbsp parsley flakes
1 tsp rosemary
1 room temperature egg

Pie Dough
1¼ cups flour
½ tsp salt
½ Tbsp thyme
½ Tbsp rosemary
6 Tbsp cold unsalted butter, cubed
¼ cup cold water

INSTRUCTIONS

1 Preheat oven to 400°F. Combine all filling ingredients in a large bowl; stir until the vegetables are evenly coated with the olive oil. Line a baking sheet with tinfoil and evenly spread out the vegetables on it. Roast for 45 minutes, stirring halfway through. At the 15-minute mark, prick the red potatoes from the binding mix 4–5 times with a fork and place them on the baking sheet with the vegetables for the remaining cook time.

2 While you wait, make the pie dough. In a medium bowl, stir together all the pie dough ingredients except the butter and water. Cut the butter into the flour mix with a fork. Stir in water 1 tablespoon at a time with the fork until the mix holds together when pressed with fingers but isn't soggy. Gather it into a ball and flatten into a 4½-inch disk. Wrap the disk in plastic and freeze 15–20 minutes or until firm but not hard.

3 Roll the dough out on a floured surface until it reaches 12 inches across (if the dough is too stiff to roll, work it with your hands until it becomes pliable). Line a pie plate with the dough. Trim the edges and decorate if desired.

4   Remove the vegetables from the oven. Mash the red potatoes in a large bowl and stir in all the other binding mix ingredients. Stir the roasted vegetables into the binding mix 1 cup at a time. Pour the mix into the pie crust.

5   Bake for 15 minutes at 400°F. Turn the oven down to 350°F and bake another 25–30 minutes or until the crust and top of the pie begin to lightly brown.

Slice and serve warm to the wonderful beasts of Redwall!

delicious avalon apple tart

from *Vita Merlini* by Geoffrey of Monmouth

Makes 1 8-inch tart

"The island of apples ... gets its name from the fact that it produces all things of itself ... Of its own accord it produces grain and grapes, and apple trees grow in its woods from the close-clipped grass ..."

This savory tribute to Avalon's namesake fruit is filled with Gala apples, acorn squash, and pearl onions topped with Welsh Cheddar cheese. The rustic style and hearty flavors combine to make a side dish reminiscent of King Arthur's grand medieval feasts.

INGREDIENTS

Pie Crust
- 1¼ cups flour
- ½ tsp salt
- ½ Tbsp thyme
- ½ Tbsp rosemary
- 6 Tbsp unsalted butter, chilled and cubed
- ¼ cup cold water

Filling
- 12 pearl onions
- 3 oz Welsh or Irish white Cheddar cheese
- ½ Gala apple
- ½ lb acorn squash
- 1½ Tbsp olive oil
- ¼ tsp each salt and pepper

INSTRUCTIONS

1 To make the pie crust, stir together the flour, salt, and herbs in a medium-sized bowl. With a fork or pastry blender, cut the butter into the flour mix until the mix has a crumb-like texture with bits of pea-sized butter throughout. With a fork, stir in water 1 tablespoon at a time until the mix just holds together when pressed with fingers (but isn't soggy).

2 Form the dough into a ball. Flatten and shape it into a 4½-inch disk. Wrap the disk in plastic and freeze 15–20 minutes or until firm but not hard.

3 While you wait for the dough, start on your filling. Cut the onions in half and remove the peel from the outside. Cut the cheese into 1-inch squares. Cut the apple into 8 wedges approximately ¾-inch thick. Cut the squash in half, remove seeds and pulp, and cut into 8 wedges, the same thickness as the apples. Combine all in a medium bowl and toss with olive oil, salt, and pepper.

4 Preheat oven to 400°F. Roll out the dough on a floured surface until it reaches 12 inches across (if the dough is too stiff to roll, work it with your hands until it is pliable). Starting 2 inches from the edge of the dough, alternate placing slices of squash, apple, and onion in concentric circles until you reach the center of the dough. Tuck cheese squares between the slices.

5 Fold and pleat the edges of the dough over the outer edge of the filling, allowing the folds to be rough and uneven for a rustic look.

6 Bake 45–55 minutes until the filling is tender and the crust has begun to turn golden brown.

Serve during an Arthurian feast!

devils on horseback: bacon-wrapped dates

from *The Phantom of the Opera* by Gaston Leroux

Makes 18 bacon-wrapped dates

*"I knew what he had made of a certain palace at Mazenderan.
From being the most honest building conceivable, he soon turned it into
a house of the very devil, where you could not utter a word but it was
overheard or repeated by an echo. With his trap-doors the monster
was responsible for endless tragedies of all kinds."*
—The Persian

"Devils on Horseback" is the alternative name for bacon-wrapped dates, a common and beloved hors d'oeuvres. Delightfully elegant yet simple to make, these sweet and salty nibbles are sure to capture everyone's heart—phantoms included!

INGREDIENTS

12 strips of bacon (regular, not thick-cut)
1 12-oz package of whole Medjool dates with pits (approximately 18 dates)*

Tea pairing

Masquerade Tea, p. 123

* We're using dates that contain pits for this recipe because they are larger than pre-pitted dates even after the pit has been manually removed.

INSTRUCTIONS

1   Preheat oven to 350°F. Line a baking sheet with tinfoil and set aside. Cut a slit down the side of each date and ease out the pit with the end of your knife (don't worry about ruining the date; this isn't a delicate procedure).

2   Slice the bacon strips width-wise into thirds. Wrap one piece around each date with the seam on top. Wrap another piece over the top of each date, with the seam on the bottom.

3   Place your bacon-wrapped dates in rows on the baking sheet and bake for 30–40 minutes or until the bacon is crisp. Allow to rest on top of the stove for 5–10 minutes to cool slightly.

Serve warm to the mysterious inhabitant of the catacombs under the Paris Opera House!

hannah's muffs: sweet potato bacon pastries

from *Little Women* by Louisa May Alcott

Makes 9 muffs

"These turnovers were an institution, and the girls called them 'muffs,' for they had no others and found the hot pies very comforting to their hands on cold mornings."

In *Little Women*, Hannah's famed "muffs" are savory turnovers. The filling is never revealed, but simple foods like sweet potatoes were common fare for the Marches . . . and if I know good-hearted Hannah, she wouldn't be able to resist sneaking in a treat like bacon!

INGREDIENTS

3 strips bacon
1 sweet potato
3 oz Brie cheese
2 sheets frozen puff
   pastry, thawed
1 egg whisked with
   1 tsp water
¼ tsp kosher salt,
   for dusting

Tea pairing

Jo's Gingerbread
Tea, p. 122

INSTRUCTIONS

1 Preheat oven to 400°F. Line a baking sheet with parchment paper and set aside. Fry the bacon and set on a paper towel–lined plate to drain.

2 Peel the sweet potato and slice it into ¼-inch-thick disks (trim each disk if necessary to make sure it is no wider than 2 inches). Cut the bacon into 1½-inch pieces. Cut the rind from the Brie.

3 Cut the pastry into 3-inch circles (you should get 9 circles from each sheet). Lay half of the circles on the baking sheet. Place 1 piece of potato on each circle. Spread on enough Brie to cover the sweet potato. Top with bacon. Brush the edges of each pastry with the egg wash.

4 Gently stretch the remaining circles slightly to make them a little larger and lay them on top of the filling. Press the edges down to seal. Brush the tops with egg wash and prick 3 times with a fork. Sprinkle with salt.

5 Bake for 15 minutes or until golden brown on top.

Serve to the March sisters to keep them warm on winter walks!

haycorns for piglet

from *Winnie-the-Pooh* by A. A. Milne

Makes 15 haycorns

"I'm planting a haycorn, Pooh, so that it can grow up into an oak-tree, and have lots of haycorns just outside the front door instead of having to walk miles and miles. Do you see, Pooh?"
—Piglet

Piglet is one of my favorite fiction characters because he shows that greatness can come in a tiny package. Let's show our appreciation for Piglet by making his favorite food: haycorns! Of course, actual acorns aren't that palatable, but these cheese-based reproductions are just the thing to start a culinary journey through the Hundred Acre Wood.

INGREDIENTS

3 oz Asiago cheese
4 spreadable Swiss cheese wedges (0.75 oz each)
¼ cup sliced almonds

Special Tools
Piping bag fitted with a large round tip

Step 3

INSTRUCTIONS

1   Finely shred the Asiago. In a medium bowl, mix the Asiago and cheese wedges until well combined. Cover and chill for 30 minutes.

2   Preheat oven to 325°F. Spread the almonds out on an ungreased baking sheet and toast for 3–5 minutes or until just slightly brown. Allow to cool, then gather them together in the middle of the pan and finely crush with a rolling pin. Set aside.

3   Line a baking sheet with parchment or wax paper. Scoop the cheese mix into a piping bag fitted with a large round tip. Using a spiral motion, pipe the mix into small cone shapes (approximately ½ tablespoon per cone). Smooth them with your finger using a downward swiping motion and pinch the tip to get the desired acorn shape.

4   Lightly drape with plastic wrap and chill for another 30 minutes.

5   Roll the bottoms in crushed almonds to make the acorn cap. Make sure the bottoms are thoroughly coated, since this is what keeps the haycorns from sticking to the serving plate.

Serve while spending time with your favorite Very Small Animal!

Tea pairing

Hundred Acre Tea, p. 121

miss marple's "pocket full of rye" tea sandwiches

from *A Pocket Full of Rye* by Agatha Christie

Makes 9 small sandwiches

"She may have accused Crump, you know. And then he lost his head and perhaps managed to put something in the sandwiches and Gladys saw him do it . . ."
—Mrs. Percival

These delicious rye sandwiches come in three classic teatime varieties: cucumber with herbed butter, homemade egg salad, and smoked salmon with caper-onion cream cheese. They're traditional enough for Miss Marple's tastes but substantial enough to revitalize you after a hard day's sleuthing.

INGREDIENTS

1 mini cucumber
¾ tsp nonpareil capers
1 Tbsp red onion, finely chopped
4 oz softened cream cheese
15 slices rye bread
4 Tbsp herbed butter*
½ cup egg salad (for recipe, see p. 41)
2–3 slices smoked salmon

INSTRUCTIONS

1   Slice the cucumber into thin disks and set aside. Mix the capers and onion into the cream cheese until well combined. Set aside.

2   Trim the crust from the bread. Cut 6 of the slices into squares, 6 into circles, and the final 3 into rectangles. Then cut the 3 rectangles into 6 triangles by slicing them in half diagonally. This will leave you with enough triangles, circles, and squares to make 3 sandwiches of each shape.

Tea pairing

Poirot's Chocoate Mate Tea, p. 124

* To make, mix 1 tsp fresh or dried herb of your choice into softened butter until combined.

3 Spread the herbed butter on the triangles and cream cheese mix on the squares. Top half the triangles with cucumber slices and half the squares with pieces of salmon, trimmed to fit. Spoon egg salad onto half of the circles.

4 Place the remaining bread shapes on top.

Serve for afternoon tea after a thrilling murder investigation!

mr. and mrs. beaver's ham sandwiches

from *The Lion, the Witch, and the Wardrobe* by C. S. Lewis

Makes 6 swiss-rolled sandwiches

"So down the steep bank they went and back to the cave, and Mr. Beaver cut some of the bread and ham into sandwiches and Mrs. Beaver poured out the tea and everyone enjoyed themselves. But long before they had finished enjoying themselves Mr. Beaver said, 'Time to be moving on now.'"

These sandwiches are deceptively simple. Despite their elegant Swiss roll appearance, each one takes less than 3 minutes to construct. The unique flavor profile makes them just as much fun to eat as to make!

INGREDIENTS

6 slices of bread*
2 oz cream cheese
6 Tbsp pesto
6 slices prosciutto

* Oatmeal bread and potato bread work well for this recipe, since the higher moisture content makes them easy to roll without tearing.

NOTE: Try not to wait for more than a few hours before serving, as the moisture from the pesto can begin to soften the bread.

INSTRUCTIONS

1   Roll both sides of each bread slice flat with a rolling pin. With a sharp knife, trim away the crust.

2   Spread a thin layer of cream cheese over one side of each slice, making sure to coat the bread right up to the edges.

3   Starting from a short end, spread on a thin layer of pesto, but stop when you get ½-inch away from the other end (this will allow the exposed cream cheese to act as a glue holding the finished sandwich together). Add your prosciutto, trimming it if necessary to prevent it from extending beyond the pesto. When you're finished, you should have all your fillings in place, with a ½-inch-wide line of exposed cream cheese down one side.

4   Starting from the side opposite the cream cheese line, roll your bread tightly enough for the spiral to keep its form but not so tight that you tear the bread.

5   Trim the round ends on each sandwich to better showcase the fillings inside.

6   Wrap the rolls tightly in plastic wrap and place in an airtight container in the fridge until ready to serve.

Serve while lunching with Mr. and Mrs. Beaver!

panther's pasties

from *Alice's Adventures in Wonderland* by Lewis Carroll

Makes 28 pasties

*"The Panther took pie-crust, and gravy, and meat,
While the Owl had the dish as its share of the treat."*

These delicious beef and potato pasties are just the right size for serving with tea. They're also a great way to use leftover pot roast—just dice up your leftovers, mix in some gravy, scoop onto your puff pastry squares, and bake!

INGREDIENTS

2 cups stew beef
2 carrots
2 stalks celery
½ sweet onion
1 baking potato
5 Tbsp beef gravy
1 Tbsp snipped
   fresh parsley
¼ tsp dried rosemary
½ tsp salt
¼ tsp pepper
4 sheets frozen puff
   pastry, thawed
1 egg, lightly beaten

INSTRUCTIONS

1 Preheat oven to 450°F.

2 Sear the stew beef and let it rest for 5 minutes. Cut into 1-inch cubes.

3 Coarsely chop your carrots, celery, and onion. Peel and cut your potato into ½-inch cubes. Microwave carrots on high for 1 minute and potatoes for 2 minutes.

4 Combine the beef, vegetables, gravy, herbs, and spices into a medium bowl. Stir to combine.

5 Cut the puff pastry into 3-inch squares. Add a spoonful of meat mix to the center of each square. Pinch the corners of each square together to create raised sides.

6 Brush with the beaten egg. Place the pasties on greased baking sheets and bake for 10 minutes or until the edges begin to brown.

7 Remove to a wire rack to cool for 5 minutes.

Serve warm at a mad tea party!

phantom's savory apple rose tartlets

from *The Phantom of the Opera* by Gaston Leroux

Makes 12 tartlets

"Why, he leaves them on the little shelf in the box, of course. I find them with the program, which I always give him. Some evenings, I find flowers in the box, a rose that must have dropped from his lady's bodice . . . for he brings a lady with him sometimes; one day, they left a fan behind them."
—Mme. Giry

Roses are known to be the Phantom's calling card, so you're sure to win him over with these savory Gouda and caramelized onion tartlets, topped with apple rosettes.

INGREDIENTS

2 batches pie dough (see recipe, p. 23)
½ Vidalia onion
1 Tbsp olive oil
½ tsp salt
¼ tsp sugar
2.5 oz Gouda cheese
2–3 Gala or Fuji apples*
Lemon juice

Special Tools
Mandoline

* You want the reddest ones you can find, since these will be sliced very thin to make rose petals. Bright red apples ensure clean red lines along the edges of the finished rosettes.

INSTRUCTIONS

1 Preheat oven to 350°F. Roll the pie dough to ⅛-inch thickness on a floured surface and cut into 4½-inch circles.

2 Thoroughly coat a muffin pan with cooking spray and gently lower the circles into the muffin wells. Prick the bottoms twice with a fork. Blind bake the circles for 10 minutes. Allow to rest until completely cool (do not remove them from the muffin pan).

3 While you wait for the shells to cool, cut your onion into thin disks. Heat the olive oil in a large skillet on medium-low heat. Add the onions, stirring them around until completely coated with oil. Cover and allow to cook for 15–20 minutes until soft and translucent, stirring occasionally.

4 Turn up the heat to medium-high and stir in the sugar and salt. Continue to cook and stir until the onions are golden brown. Remove from heat and set aside.

5 Cut the Gouda into 12 disks approximately ¼-inch thick and 2 inches wide. Use them to line the bottom of the tart shells. For an easier but less exact alternative, cut the Gouda into small chunks and evenly distribute them between the tart shells.

6 Place pieces of onion equivalent to 1–2 full rings on top of each Gouda disk.

7 Cut the apples into quarters and cut out the seeded portions. Slice the quarters thin using the second setting on a mandoline. As you cut, place the finished slices in a bowl and toss them with a few drops of lemon juice every so often to prevent browning.

8   Squirt some lemon juice on a cutting board and line up 10 apple slices overlapping each other in a straight line. Slowly roll the slices into a spiral, making sure to keep a good grip on the outside apples. For the most success with your apple roses, place each apple slice so that it lays halfway over the previous slice (this will provide structural stability). If the slices are thinner at one end, face the thin end toward the outside of the overlap (this will make rolling easier). Angle each slice just slightly downward, so that when you roll it up, the "petals" in the center will be higher, providing a more authentic rose look.

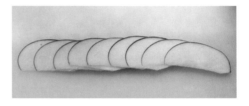

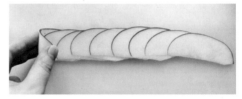

NOTE: If your apple slices are breaking as you roll them, you may be rolling too tightly. Try rolling the first few slices loosely, leaving a hole in the middle of your finished rose. Then tuck an extra slice or two in the middle after you place it in the tart.

9   Place the rolled rose in the center of one of the tart shells, pressing down to make sure it holds its shape. Repeat with all the remaining apple slices.

10   Bake for 10–15 minutes, until the apple slices are cooked through and the cheese has had time to melt. Keep a close watch on them for the last few minutes to make sure the edges of the petals don't start to burn.

11   Allow the tartlets to rest for 5 minutes in the pan, then ease them out with a butter knife onto a serving plate.

Serve a dozen or so of these delicious roses to the love of your life!

poetical egg salad sandwiches

from *Anne of Avonlea* by L. M. Montgomery

Makes 6 sandwiches

"Little jelly tarts and lady fingers, and drop cookies frosted with pink and yellow icing, and buttercup cake. And we must have sandwiches too, though they're not very poetical."
—Anne

Leave it to Anne Shirley to turn an egg salad sandwich into a feast for the imagination. As I recreated the sandwiches she served to her friends during their "golden picnic," I resolved to make them as Anne would: with as much extra flair as possible. These sandwiches start with watercress-lined croissants and are filled with egg salad (with an added secret ingredient!). The result was a feast for kings, no imagination necessary!

INGREDIENTS

1 dozen hard boiled eggs*
3 sticks imitation crab
1 cup mayonnaise
1½ Tbsp mustard
½ tsp salt
1 tsp parsley flakes
1 tsp chives
6 large croissants
1 bunch fresh watercress

INSTRUCTIONS

1 Shell and coarsely chop the eggs. Chop your crab into slightly smaller pieces than the eggs.

2 In a large bowl, combine the eggs, crab, mayonnaise, mustard, salt, parsley, and chives. Stir to combine.

3 Cut the croissants in half lengthwise and place a layer of watercress leaves on the bottom half of each croissant.

4 Spoon a generous helping of egg salad over the watercress and place the second half of croissant on top.

Serve during a golden picnic in Avonlea!

Tea pairing

Raspberry Cordial
Tea, p. 125

* For technique, see
p. 21.

NOTE: If reheating these in the microwave, cut them in half before heating (microwaved eggs can explode, even if pricked with a fork).

scotch eggs

from *The Horse and His Boy* by C. S. Lewis

Makes 6 Scotch eggs

"By the time Shasta had finished his porridge, the Dwarf's two brothers (whose names were Rogin and Bricklethumb) were putting the dish of bacon and eggs and mushrooms, and the coffee pot and the hot milk, and the toast, on the table."

Inspired by the Narnian dwarves' preferred traveling snacks, these eggs combine three breakfast favorites—eggs, bacon, and sausage—to make a truly hearty start to any day.

INGREDIENTS

7 large eggs
1½ tsp salt, divided
¾ cup Panko crumbs
12 oz finely ground
   breakfast sausage
½ Tbsp finely chopped
   green onion
1 Tbsp bacon bits
¼ tsp pepper
4–6 cups vegetable oil

Step 4

INSTRUCTIONS

1   Lightly beat 1 egg and set aside. Add the remaining eggs to a pot with 1 teaspoon salt. Fill the pot with water until the eggs are covered and place it over medium heat. When the water begins to boil, remove it from heat and cover for 6–8 minutes. Drain and rinse the eggs in cold water repeatedly until they reach room temperature. Peel and discard the shells.

2   Place the beaten egg and Panko crumbs in 2 separate bowls. Remove the sausage from its casing and add it to a medium-sized bowl. Knead the green onion, bacon bits, ½ teaspoon salt, and pepper into the sausage.

3   Heat the oil in a large pot until sizzling.

4   While the oil heats, wrap the eggs as thinly as possible in the sausage. Do this by dividing the sausage mix into 6 equal pieces and shaping these into balls. Flatten a ball in your palm. Place an egg in the center and press the sausage around the egg until completely encased. Repeat for all the remaining eggs. Roll the sausage-wrapped eggs in the beaten egg. Then roll them in the Panko crumbs.

5   Lower 2–3 eggs into the oil and cook 2–3 minutes or until golden brown (cut into the sausage layer of 1 egg to check for doneness). Remove the eggs with a slotted spoon or tongs and set them on a paper towel–lined plate to drain for 5 minutes.

6   Repeat Step 5 with the remaining eggs.

Serve warm on a cold winter's day in Narnia!

sherlock's steak sandwiches

from "The Adventure of the Beryl Coronet" by Sir Arthur Conan Doyle

Makes 2 large sandwiches (these can be cut into halves or quarters
for teatime-sized portions)

*"He cut a slice of beef from the joint upon the sideboard, sandwiched it
between two rounds of bread, and thrusting this rude meal into
his pocket he started off upon his expedition."*

Sherlock Holmes is famous for having a sparse appetite, but cold beef sandwiches seem to be a weakness of his. He indulges in them several times throughout the books, mostly while traveling on a case. I can see why! What could be better brain food that hearty bread, protein that sticks to your ribs, and some choice toppings to awaken your taste buds?

INGREDIENTS

Sauce
3 Tbsp sour cream
2 Tbsp horseradish sauce
1 strong pinch kosher salt
1 strong dash
   black pepper
¾ tsp lemon juice

Sandwiches
½ lb boneless steak, cut
   into 2 portions*
Salt and pepper, to taste
4 slices whole
   wheat bread
4 radishes
1½ cups arugula

Tea pairing

Deduction: A
Sherlock Tea, p. 120

INSTRUCTIONS

1 Mix all the sauce ingredients together in a small bowl. Set aside.

2 Season the steak with salt and pepper to taste. Lightly oil a skillet and set on medium heat. When the skillet is hot, sear the steak for 2 minutes on both sides. Hold the short ends down on the skillet with a pair of tongs for 10 seconds each, just long enough to seal in the juices. Set the steak aside on a plate to rest.

3 Toast the bread. Thinly slice the radishes to about ¼-inch thickness.

4 Spread sauce on a slice of bread and arrange some arugula on top (this will act as a moisture barrier against the meat). Place the slices from one radish on top. Slice the steak into ½-inch wide strips and place half of them on top of the radish layer. Add another layer of radish and then more arugula. Spread sauce on another piece of bread and place it on top.

5 Repeat Step 4 for the second sandwich.

6 Cut the sandwiches into halves or quarters if desired.

Pack them to go as you run off to break the case!

* The sandwiches pictured use boneless chuck eye steak.

stuffed button mushrooms

from *Alice's Adventures in Wonderland* by Lewis Carroll

Makes 12 stuffed button mushrooms

"Then [the caterpillar] got down off the mushroom, and crawled away into the grass, merely remarking as it went, 'One side will make you grow taller, and the other side will make you grow shorter.'"

These elegant stuffed mushrooms feature three kinds of cheese: Ricotta and Parmesan filling with Cheddar cheese crisps on top!

INGREDIENTS

¾ cup whole milk ricotta
1 egg
1 Tbsp chopped
    green onion
1 Tbsp Parmesan cheese
⅛ tsp salt
⅛ tsp pepper
12 white
    button mushrooms
1 Tbsp finely shredded
    sharp Cheddar cheese

INSTRUCTIONS

1 Preheat oven to 350°F.

2 In a medium-sized bowl, stir the ricotta and egg until combined. Stir in green onion, Parmesan cheese, salt, and pepper.

3 Remove the stems from the bottom of the mushrooms either by twisting or pushing the base of the stem gently on one side. Discard the stems or save them for soup.

4 Place the mushrooms on a baking sheet and spoon in the filling (about 2 teaspoons each, depending on the size of the mushroom).

5 Place the baking sheet in the oven and bake for 12 minutes. Be careful not to leave them in too long or the bottoms of the mushrooms can begin to leak.

6 While you wait for the mushrooms to cook, spread the Cheddar cheese in a 3½-inch circle in the bottom of a small skillet. Heat the skillet on low until the cheese is barely bubbling and the edges just begin to brown (3–5 minutes). Set the cheese disk on a paper towel–lined plate for 5–10 minutes to cool.

7 Break the cheese disk into 12 pieces and set a piece on top of each mushroom.

Serve to a mysterious caterpillar you meet in Wonderland!

sword in the stone cheese bites

from *The Story of King Arthur and His Knights* by Howard Pyle

Makes 16 cheese bites

"Thereupon Arthur went to the cube of marble stone and he laid his hands upon the haft of the sword . . . And he bent his body and drew very strongly and, lo! the sword came forth with great ease and very smoothly."

These easy, delicious cheese bites are just the right snack to kick off a long afternoon of knightly adventuring . . . or at least reading about knightly adventures! The perfect combo of Camembert and English Cheddar is balanced with toasted nuts and sweet-tart dried cranberries—a truly kingly dish!

INGREDIENTS

- 2 oz white English Cheddar
- 8 oz Camembert
- 2 Tbsp dried cranberries
- 2 Tbsp pecan or walnut chips, toasted
- ¼ tsp fresh ground pepper

Special Tools
- 16 plastic cocktail swords

INSTRUCTIONS

1 In a medium bowl, finely shred the Cheddar and scoop the Camembert cheese from inside its rind, discarding the rind. Stir all the ingredients together until well combined. Cover tightly with plastic wrap and chill for 25–30 minutes or until firm.

2 Remove the plastic wrap and roll the cheese mix into balls approximately 1¼ inches across.

3 Insert the cocktail swords into the top of each ball.

Serve to the bravest knights in all the land!

> **NOTE:** If you like, you can roll the cheese balls in 2 tablespoons of poppy seeds before inserting the cocktail swords for a more authentic "stone" look.

bread & muffins

Many of us appreciate the simple wholesomeness of bread, but few realize how authors often use it to illustrate the relationships between characters. If we pay close attention, we'll notice that bread in books is rarely eaten alone. Instead, it is almost always shared, be it among family at a dinner table or fireside companions on a lonely trail.

Beorn the bear man from *The Hobbit* is a great example. Though he initially has no love for the outside world, he takes Bilbo and his companions into his home and shares homemade bread along with honey from his own hives.

Beorn begins to recognize the duty that all people have to care for each other, which is why he joins the Battle of the Five Armies later in the book, despite his original desire to remain secluded. Beorn shows us that our responsibility for each other is as fundamental as the bread we share.

arctic trail coffee muffins

from *White Fang* by Jack London

Makes 12 muffins

"Henry did not reply, but munched on in silence, until, the meal finished, he topped it with a final cup of coffee. He wiped his mouth with the back of his hand . . . A long wailing cry, fiercely sad, from somewhere in the darkness, had interrupted him."

With a little maple butter, these make the perfect breakfast. To make your own maple butter, simply mix a few tablespoons of maple syrup into a stick of softened butter until smooth.

INGREDIENTS

½ cup unsalted butter
2 tsp instant
  coffee granules
1 cup milk
2 cups flour
½ cup granulated sugar
¼ cup brown sugar
2 tsp baking powder
¼ tsp each cinnamon,
  ginger, and nutmeg
½ tsp salt
2 Tbsp maple syrup
1 egg
1 tsp vanilla extract

INSTRUCTIONS

1 Preheat oven to 375°F. Melt the butter in a microwave and set aside to cool. Stir the instant coffee granules into the milk and allow to dissolve. Fill a muffin pan with liners and set aside.

2 In a large bowl, whisk together the flour, sugars, baking powder, spices, and salt. Whisk in the syrup, egg, vanilla, melted butter, and milk mix (stir the milk thoroughly before pouring it in).

3 Fill the muffin liners ¾ full. Bake for 20 minutes or until a toothpick inserted in the center comes out clean. Remove the muffins from the pan and allow to cool for 20 minutes on a wire rack.

Serve warm on a cold Alaskan morning!

beorn's honey nut banana bread

from *The Hobbit* by J. R. R. Tolkien

Makes 1 loaf

"[Beorn] lives in an oak-wood and has a great wooden house; and as a man he keeps cattle and horses which are nearly as marvelous as himself. They work for him and talk to him . . . He keeps hives and hives of great fierce bees; and lives most on cream and honey."
—Gandalf

Beorn may be a tough nut to crack, but he can make a mean meal! Below is my own interpretation of the bread and honey he serves Thorin's company when they stay at his home on the edge of Mirkwood Forest.

INGREDIENTS

1¼ cups flour
½ tsp baking soda
⅛ tsp salt
¼ tsp cinnamon
¼ tsp ginger
2 brown bananas
¼ cup granulated sugar
¼ cup brown sugar
3 Tbsp honey
½ tsp vanilla extract
1 egg, lightly beaten
¼ cup melted butter, cooled
¼ cup walnut chips

INSTRUCTIONS

1 Preheat oven to 350°F. Coat a loaf pan with cooking spray and set aside.

2 In a large bowl, whisk together flour, baking soda, salt, cinnamon, and ginger. Create a well in the center of the flour mix. Set aside.

3 In a medium bowl, mash the bananas with a fork. Stir in the sugars, honey, vanilla, egg, and melted butter.

4 Add the wet mix to the well in the center of the dry mix. Stir until just combined. Stir in the walnuts.

5 Pour the mix into the loaf pan and bake for 45 minutes or until a toothpick inserted in the center comes out clean.

6 Allow to cool in the pan for 10 minutes. Loosen the loaf from the pan along the edges with a butter knife and overturn the loaf onto a wire rack. Allow to rest upright until completely cool (approximately 1 hour).

7 Wrap the loaf in plastic wrap and store at room temperature for 1 day before serving.

Tea pairing

Bilbo's Breakfast Brew, p. 120

Serve to a disgruntled shapeshifter to thank him for protecting you from goblins!

Tea pairing

Princess Sara's Chocolate Chai, p. 124

blackberry lemon sweet rolls

from *A Little Princess* by Frances Hodgson Burnett

Makes 18 sweet rolls

"She looked straight at the shop directly facing her. And it was a baker's shop, and a cheerful, stout, motherly woman with rosy cheeks was putting into the window a tray of delicious newly baked hot buns, fresh from the oven . . ."

When Sara Crewe is suddenly thrown into poverty, she struggles with hunger every day. One day, she finds a coin in the street and uses it to buy six warm, fresh bakery buns. Then the baker woman sees her give five of them away to a starving child on the street! The baker is so touched by Sara's generosity, she takes in the child Sara helped and teaches her to work in the bakery. Sara shows us all that a simple act of generosity can start a chain reaction that changes lives.

INGREDIENTS

Rolls
¼ cup very warm water
½ cup room
   temperature milk
1 packet (7 grams) active
   dry yeast
¼ cup butter, softened
2 tsp vanilla extract
½ tsp salt
¼ cup sugar
2 eggs
2¾ cups flour
¾ cup seedless
   blackberry
   spreadable fruit

Icing
½ cup powdered sugar
1 Tbsp milk
½ tsp lemon extract
2–3 tsp lemon zest

Special Tools
A long piece of clean
   floss or thin string

INSTRUCTIONS

1 Stir together the water and milk in the bowl of a standing mixer. Sprinkle the yeast on top and allow to sit for 5 minutes.

2 Add the butter, vanilla, salt, sugar, and 1 egg to the bowl. Beat on medium-low speed with a paddle attachment for 30 seconds or until the butter is broken up into pieces.

3 Gradually beat in the flour on medium speed until just combined.

4 Turn the dough out onto a floured surface and knead until it is soft, mostly smooth, and only slightly sticky (approximately 5–8 minutes). You may need to periodically reflour the surface to keep the dough from sticking.

5 Coat a large bowl with cooking spray and place the dough inside, turning once to coat. Cover the bowl with a clean kitchen cloth and allow to rise for 1 hour or until the dough has roughly doubled in size.

6 Preheat oven to 350°F. Coat two muffin pans with cooking spray and set aside.

7 Punch down the dough and roll it out into a 15x10-inch rectangle on a floured surface. Coat the dough in an even layer of the spreadable fruit. Starting from the narrow end, loosely roll the dough into a swiss roll.

8 Using a piece of clean floss or thin string, cut the roll into 1-inch-thick disks by sliding the middle of the floss under the dough 1 inch from the end, crossing the two ends over the top, and pulling the ends in opposite directions. They should cut into the dough and slice a disk off the end with the shape of the spiral still preserved.

9 Place the disks into the muffin pans with the "cleaner" side (the side that shows less jam) facing upward. Beat the remaining egg and brush it onto the disks. Bake for 10–15 minutes or until the rolls have risen and are golden brown along the edges, swapping and turning the pans once halfway through. Allow to rest for 5 minutes in the pan, then ease them out with a butter knife and transfer to a wire rack to cool completely.

10 Stir your powdered sugar, milk, and lemon extract together until smooth. Drizzle it over the top of the buns and sprinkle the zest on top.

Serve to hungry passersby on the streets of London!

NOTE: Cutting the buns from the roll can get a bit messy, but doing it on a cutting board will save you from having to clean jam off your counter.

blood orange scones

from "The Five Orange Pips" by Arthur Conan Doyle

Makes 8 scones

"Opening [the envelope] hurriedly, out there jumped five little dried orange pips, which pattered down upon his plate."

This reinterpretation of the classic British scone is inspired by "The Five Orange Pips," one of Sherlock Holmes' most difficult cases. Luckily, this citrusy scone is delicious enough to make you forget even your peskiest case. The outside has a firm, sweet crust, and the inside is tender with a distinct orange flavor. This recipe uses blood orange bitters instead of juice, which means you can make it even if blood oranges aren't in season!

INGREDIENTS

2 cups flour
¼ cup sugar, plus ¾ tsp for dusting
2 tsp baking powder
½ tsp baking soda
½ tsp salt
⅓ cup cold butter, divided into tablespoons
1 Tbsp orange zest (or blood orange zest, if they're in season)
1 egg, lightly beaten
¼ cup blood orange bitters
¼ cup cold half and half
1 Tbsp milk, for brushing on top

Tea pairing

Deduction: A Sherlock Tea, p. 120

INSTRUCTIONS

1 Preheat oven to 425°F. Line a baking sheet with parchment paper and set aside.

2 Whisk the flour, ¼ cup sugar, baking powder, baking soda, and salt together in a large bowl. With a fork or pastry blender, cut the butter into the flour mix until the mix has a crumb-like texture with bits of pea-sized butter throughout. Stir in the zest and make a well in the center of the flour mix.

3 Add the beaten egg to the well. Mix the bitters and half and half together. Pour that into the well also. Stir it all up with a fork until just combined. The dough will be damp and a little sticky (don't work it too much, because that can make the scones tough).

4 Shape the dough into a ball with your hands, making sure to press any stray bits from the bottom of the bowl into the ball. Place it on the prepared baking sheet and flatten it into a 7½–8-inch round disk. Use a sharp knife to score the disk into triangles. Cut about halfway through the dough to ensure that the lines don't disappear while baking (cutting halfway through without completely separating allows the scones to retain more moisture than if they were baked as individual triangles, while still keeping the lines of the individual portions visible).

5 Brush the top of the dough with milk and sprinkle on ¾ teaspoon sugar.

...plants in hybrid...

den and extreme

...face worn at a carnival. masquerad...

monster (mon-ster) *n.* a legendary
combining features of animal and
form or having the forms of vario
animals in combination. as a centa
griffin. or sphinx.

...moon when
d.
an.

moonlight (moon-lahyt) *n.* the lig
he moon.

...(muhn-ee) *n.* the dead b
...ng or animal preserve
...n process or some
...uming.

...od of dar

-too
ing acce
r peculiar k
p. or historical p

...muh n) *n.* a

1. coldness. especiall
t uncomfortably penetrat
a feeling of sudden fea

6 Bake for 15–20 minutes or until the center is fully set and the top is golden brown. Don't worry if the top browns well before the center is finished. The crust sets a bit early, but it shouldn't burn. Instead, keep an eye on the center. If it looks wet and uncooked, leave it in the oven. Once the center has just begun to look fully set, take it out.

7 Allow to cool on the pan for 5 minutes. When ready to serve, slice along the lines you scored earlier.

Serve warm with Devonshire cream and jam while solving a tough case!

NOTE: Blood oranges are in season from December to May.

hot cross currant buns

from *The Secret Garden* by Frances Hodgson Burnett

Makes 16 buns

"The morning that Dickon . . . went behind a big rosebush and brought forth two tin pails and revealed that one was full of rich new milk with cream on the top of it, and that the other held cottage-made currant buns folded in a clean blue and white napkin, buns so carefully tucked in that they were still hot, there was a riot of surprised joyfulness. What a wonderful thing for Mrs. Sowerby to think of!"

Currants are very similar to raisins but smaller with a slightly fruitier taste. In modern baking, currant buns appear most often in the form of hot cross buns, which are traditionally served during Easter season. This particular recipe includes chopped dried apricot for extra sweetness.

INGREDIENTS

Buns
¼ cup very warm water
½ cup room
   temperature milk
1 packet (7 grams) active
   dry yeast
¼ cup butter, softened
2 eggs
½ tsp salt
¼ tsp each ground
   cinnamon, nutmeg,
   and ginger
¼ cup sugar
2¾ cups flour
¼ cup dried currants*
¼ cup chopped
   dried apricot

Icing
1¼ cup powdered sugar
2 Tbsp milk

Special Tools
Piping bag fitted with
   ¼-inch round tip

INSTRUCTIONS

1 Stir together the water and milk in the bowl of a standing mixer. Sprinkle the yeast on top and allow to sit for 5 minutes.

2 Add the butter, 1 egg, salt, spices, and sugar to the bowl. Beat on medium-low speed with a paddle attachment for 30 seconds or until the butter is broken up into pieces.

3 Gradually beat in the flour on medium speed until just combined. Pour in all the dried fruit and beat until just combined.

4 Turn the dough out onto a floured surface and knead until it is soft, mostly smooth, and only slightly sticky (approximately 5–8 minutes). You may need to periodically reflour the surface to keep the dough from sticking.

5 Coat a large bowl with cooking spray and place the dough inside, turning once to coat. Cover the bowl with a clean kitchen cloth and allow to rise for 1 hour or until the dough has roughly doubled in size.

6 Punch down the dough and set aside. Coat two baking sheets with cooking spray and separate the dough into 16 balls of equal size, placing them an equal distance apart on the baking sheets. Cover and allow to rise for another 30 minutes.

* If you aren't a fan of the raisin flavor typically associated with currants, try substituting dried cranberries.

7   Preheat oven to 375°F. Whisk the remaining egg with 1 tablespoon water and brush the top of the balls of the first tray with egg wash. Bake for 6–8 minutes or until just beginning to turn golden brown on top. Allow to cool for 5 minutes on the baking sheet. Brush and bake the second tray, allowing to cool for 5 minutes on the tray as well. Remove buns to a wire rack to cool completely.

8   For the icing, stir together the powdered sugar and milk until smooth. Transfer to a piping bag fitted with a ¼-inch round tip and pipe a cross on top of each bun. Traditionally, the shape is closer to a plus sign (+) than a true cross.

Serve with fresh milk in a secret garden!

star-crossed focaccia with parmesan chive butter

from *Romeo and Juliet* by William Shakespeare

Makes 1 focaccia loaf and ½ cup butter

"Two households, both alike in dignity,
In fair Verona, where we lay our scene,
From ancient grudge break to new mutiny,
Where civil blood makes civil hands unclean.
From forth the fatal loins of these two foes
A pair of star-cross'd lovers take their life . . ."
—Prologue

You can cut out just a few stars for effect or cut them as close together as possible to make several stars, eating the scraps as a snack. If doing the latter, cut the stars just before serving to prevent the bread from drying out.

INGREDIENTS

Bread
1 13.8-oz can of
   pizza dough
½ tsp salt
¼ tsp black pepper
2 Tbsp pesto

Butter
½ cup butter, softened
2½ Tbsp Parmesan
2 Tbsp snipped
   fresh chives

Special Tools
3-inch star cookie cutter
Pizza stone

Step 3

INSTRUCTIONS

1   Preheat oven to 400°F. Let the dough come to room temperature.

2   Place the dough in a large bowl and knead in your salt and pepper. Tug the dough into an 8-inch circle on a pizza stone. It may try to spring back, but keep pulling and pressing at it until it stays close to 8 inches across.

3   Brush the dough with pesto. With the back of a wooden spoon or greased metal spoon, make indentations in the dough about 1 inch apart by pressing down firmly on the dough (you may need to press all the way down until you touch the pizza stone for the indentations to remain visible).

4   Bake 10–15 minutes or until the top begins to turn golden brown. While you wait, stir together the butter ingredients in a small bowl and set aside.

5   Let the bread rest on the stone for 5–10 minutes or until cool enough to handle. Move to a cutting board and cut out stars with a star cookie cutter.

Serve alongside the butter to the Fates to convince them to favor you!

toasted cheese buns

from *Treasure Island* by Robert Louis Stevenson

Makes 8 buns

*"You mightn't happen to have a piece of cheese about you, now? No?
Well, many's the long night I've dreamed of cheese—toasted mostly . . ."*
—Ben Gunn

When telling Jim Hawkins what he misses most about home, Ben Gunn waxes lyrical about cheese. If I was marooned on a deserted island for three years, I'd crave cheese, too! These buns are topped with shredded Cheddar and have green onion and garlic mixed right into the dough. Plus, they hide a delicious treasure—a melted cheese center!

INGREDIENTS

- 1 lb frozen bread dough
- 2 Tbsp chopped green onion
- 2 cloves minced garlic
- 3 oz sharp Cheddar cheese, cut into 8 cubes
- 1 Tbsp olive oil
- ¾ cup finely shredded Cheddar cheese

INSTRUCTIONS

1 Thaw the bread dough according to the package instructions. Preheat oven to 400°F. Line a baking sheet with parchment paper and set aside.

2 Knead the green onion and garlic into the bread dough until evenly incorporated. Divide the dough into 8 equal portions and pat into 2-inch balls.

3 Partially flatten the balls with your palm. Place a cheese cube in the center of each flattened ball. Wrap the ball around the cheese cube and knead slightly to seal shut.

4 Place the balls on the baking sheet. Brush the tops with olive oil. Press the shredded cheese on top.

5 Bake for 8–10 minutes or until the cheese on top is melted and the dough is firm on the outside. Allow to cool for 5 minutes on the baking sheet.

Serve while rescuing marooned pirates from a life without cheese!

sweets

From both a culinary and literary perspective, dessert adds something to meals that is nebulous and necessary: drama. We can't help but feel something when we bite into a crisp cookie or a slice of soft cake piled high with delicate frosting. Accordingly, desserts in literature are often connected to characters' emotions. In *Little Women*, Jo feels a pang of homesickness when her family sends her gingerbread during her first Christmas away from home. And candied nuts and meadowcream are always greeted with greatest joy during Redwall's many celebratory feasts.

Perhaps this is the ultimate purpose of dessert: to allow us to luxuriate in joy. Whether in real life or the pages of a book, who can resist the fun flavors, decorative appearance, and characteristic sweetness of a truly wonderful dessert?

Tea pairing

Arrietty's Cherry
Tree Tea, p. 119

arrietty's mini cherry cakes

from *The Borrowers* by Mary Norton

Makes 7 mini cakes

"Arrietty watched him move away from the step and then she looked about her. Oh, glory! Oh, joy! Oh, freedom! The sunlight, the grasses, the soft, moving air and halfway up the bank, where it curved round the corner, a flowering cherry tree! Below it on the path lay a stain of pinkish petals and, at the tree's foot, pale as butter, a nest of primroses."

The quick Devonshire cream included in this recipe is a great teatime recipe to have in your arsenal. It pairs beautifully with scones, muffins, and these lovely cherry cakes!

INGREDIENTS

1 10-oz frozen all butter pound cake
⅓ cup cherry preserves
½ cup Devonshire cream*
¼ cup powdered sugar
7 fresh cherries

Special Tools
1½–2-inch round cookie cutter

> * To make your own Devonshire cream, beat 4 oz softened cream cheese for 45 seconds in a standing mixer on medium-high speed. Add 2 Tbsp powdered sugar and 1 tsp vanilla, beating 2–3 minutes or until smooth. Gradually beat in 3 Tbsp heavy cream until the mixture is smooth and has the consistency of very dense whipped cream.

INSTRUCTIONS

1 Thaw the pound cake according to package instructions. Cut it into ½-inch-thick slices.

2 Using a round cookie cutter, cut 21 circles out of your cake slices.

3 Spread a small dollop each of cherry preserves and Devonshire cream on 14 of your 21 circles. Be careful not to spread it all the way to the edges, since the filling the will push out a little when the circles are stacked. Leave about ⅛ inch of clearance between the edge of the filling and the edge of the cake.

4 Stack the circles in towers of 3, with the plain circles (the ones without filling) on top.

5 Dust the tops of the cakes with powdered sugar. Add another small dollop of cream to the top of each cake, but don't spread it out. Set the cherries on top of the cream.

Serve under a cherry tree to your Borrower friends!

Tea pairing

Miss Mary's Garden
Blend, p. 123

candied flower cookies

from *The Secret Garden* by Frances Hodges Burnett

Makes 60 cookies

"The place was a wilderness of autumn gold and purple and violet blue and flaming scarlet . . . He remembered well when the first of them had been planted that just at this season of the year their late glories should reveal themselves."

Candied flowers may look complicated, but they're actually quite easy (though they require several hours to set). You can make the cookies using the cookie recipe provided below, or if you're pressed for time, use store-bought sugar cookies.

INGREDIENTS

Candied Flowers
2 cups pasteurized egg whites
1–2 Tbsp unflavored vodka (optional)
2 cups caster sugar*

Cookies
2 cups flour
½ tsp baking powder
¼ tsp salt
½ cup plus 2 Tbsp butter, softened
¾ cup sugar
1 egg, lightly beaten
2 Tbsp milk
2 tsp vanilla extract
1¼ cups powdered sugar icing**
60 edible flower blossoms***

Special Tools
2-inch circle cookie cutter

INSTRUCTIONS

1 Line a baking sheet with parchment paper and place the flowers in a single layer on top. In a medium bowl, whisk the egg whites until foamy. If you like, whisk vodka into the egg whites (this helps the flowers dry more quickly).

2 Completely coat the top and bottom of each flower in a thin layer of the egg foam. To do this, simply fold down most of the bristles of a pastry brush until you're left with enough bristles to act as a paintbrush, then dip the brush in the egg foam.

* To make your own caster sugar out of standard granulated sugar, simply place it in a blender or food processor and blend briefly until very fine but not powdered.

** Make by mixing 2½ cups powdered sugar with ½–1 Tbsp milk until smooth.

*** Pansies, primroses, and strawberry blossoms are all the perfect size and shape for this recipe. Be sure to use flowers that are clean and free of pesticides and chemicals.

3   After coating each flower, sprinkle on a light layer of caster sugar.

4   Allow the flowers to dry on the rack overnight (the dried flowers will be glossy, and the sugar granules will be mostly dissolved). Set the flowers aside.

5   To make the cookies, whisk together the flour, baking powder, and salt in a bowl and set aside.

6   In a standing mixer, cream together the butter and sugar on medium speed until smooth. Beat in the egg, milk, and vanilla until combined.

7   Gradually beat in the flour mix until just combined, stopping to scrape the sides of the bowl if necessary.

8   Gather the dough together into a ball. Separate into two smaller balls of equal size and wrap tightly in plastic wrap. Freeze for 15 minutes. While waiting, preheat the oven to 325°F. When the 15 minutes are up, unwrap one ball of dough and transfer the other to the fridge.

9   Generously flour a cutting board and rolling pin. Roll out the unwrapped dough to ⅛-inch thickness and cut out 15 cookies with a circle cutter (if the dough is too stiff to roll, work it with your hands until it is pliable). Place the cookies on an ungreased baking sheet an equal distance apart and bake for 8 minutes. Allow to cool on the pan for 5 minutes before moving to a wire rack to cool completely (if they seem a little stuck to the pan, gently ease them off with a butter knife). Roll out and bake another 15 circles using the scraps from the ball of dough.

10   Unwrap the second ball of dough and repeat Step 9.

11   When the cookies are cool, drizzle the icing over the cookies and place the candied flowers on top. The icing will hold them in place.

Serve at a garden party reached through a secret entrance in the garden wall!

NOTE: If you'd like to halve the recipe to make fewer cookies, use only half of the lightly beaten egg in the batter by eyeballing the amount or measuring it out with a kitchen scale. Half an egg is usually between 0.8–0.9 ounces.

cyclone cookies

from *The Wonderful Wizard of Oz* by L. Frank Baum

Makes 12 cookies

"The great pressure of the wind on every side of the house raised it up higher and higher, until it was at the very top of the cyclone; and there it remained and was carried miles and miles away as easily as you could carry a feather."

I'm crazy about the colors in these cookies. Of course, you can make them whatever color you want. Any bright, striking combination will have a fun effect!

INGREDIENTS

1 cup flour
⅛ tsp baking powder
½ cup butter, softened
¼ cup powdered sugar
¼ cup granulated sugar
¼ tsp salt
1½ tsp vanilla extract
2 Tbsp milk
3 drops each yellow, red, and blue gel coloring (or 5–7 drops each liquid food coloring)
15 drops black gel coloring (or 1 tsp liquid food coloring)

Tea pairing

Emerald City Tea, p. 121

INSTRUCTIONS

1   In a small bowl, stir together the flour and baking powder and set aside.

2   In a standing mixer, cream the butter, sugars, and salt until smooth. With the beater running, add in the vanilla and milk. Gradually beat in the flour mix until combined, stopping to scrape the sides of the bowl if necessary.

3   Scoop half of your dough out of the bowl. Divide it into thirds and place each third in a separate small bowl. Mix the yellow coloring into one bowl, red in another, and blue in the third. Shape each color of dough into a tube approximately 4 inches long. Line the tubes up against each other in a row on a sheet of wax paper. Place another sheet on top and roll to ¼-inch thickness. You want all three colors to appear in each individual cookie when you're finished, so try to roll the dough into a rectangle that has a single color on the short sides and all three colors on the long sides (this will give you enough length on the multicolored sides to create a good spiral in your cookie).

4   Add the black coloring to the dough still in the mixer and beat until the color is fully incorporated. Place the black dough between two sheets of wax paper and roll to ¼-inch thickness. Keeping the wax paper on the dough, place both sets of rolled dough on a baking sheet (setting one on top of the other is fine). Freeze for 15 minutes.

5   Remove the top sheet of wax paper from both sets of dough. Flip the black dough on top of the colored dough. Remove the second sheet of paper from the black dough. Cut the dough into a 6x8-inch rectangle (remember to cut so that the 6-inch sides are a single color and the 8-inch sides are multicolored). Starting from the short end, gently roll the rectangle into a spiral log, smoothing out any cracks with your finger as you go. Discard the final sheet of wax paper.

6 Wrap the log tightly in plastic wrap and freeze for 20 minutes. Preheat oven to 400°F.

7 Slice the log into disks that are a little under ½-inch thick. Place the disks on an ungreased baking sheet and bake for 8–10 minutes or until the edges are set. Allow the cookies to cool on the baking sheet for 5 minutes.

8 Remove to a wire rack and allow to cool completely.

Serve as you ride the cyclone to Oz!

candied nuts with meadowcream

from *The Legend of Luke: A Tale of Redwall* by Brian Jacques

Makes 1 cup chopped nuts and 3½ cups cream

*"Gnoff indicated a spot on the butter-colored meadowcream, between
a candied chestnut and a honey-preserved rose petal . . . Columbine
took over the slicing and Cogs served drinks, whilst Martin sat in
a corner with some of his friends, eating and sipping happily."*

Most Redwall recipes are simple, rustic dishes, and dessert is no exception. In fact, sugar doesn't even make an appearance in this recipe. Instead, lightly honeyed spiced walnuts are the star of this dish, accompanied by a generous helping of Redwall's famous meadowcream. This dessert's cozy flavors and homey feel make it a perfect Redwall dish!

INGREDIENTS

Nuts
1 cup chopped walnuts
3 Tbsp honey
½ tsp apple pie spice
¼ tsp salt
¼ tsp vanilla extract

Cream
1½ cups whipping cream
3 Tbsp honey

Tea pairing

Abbot's Chocolate
Hazelnut Tea, p. 119

INSTRUCTIONS

1   Preheat the oven to 325°F. Line a baking sheet with tinfoil and coat the foil with cooking spray. Set aside.

2   Add all the nut ingredients to a medium bowl and stir until well combined. Spread the mix onto the tinfoil in a thin layer, breaking up the clumps as much as possible.

3   Bake for 10 minutes, stirring once halfway through.

4   Allow the nuts to cool on the pan (approximately 15 minutes). The coating on the nuts will harden.

5   While you wait, make the meadowcream by adding the whipping cream to the bowl of a standing mixer and beating on medium-high speed for a few minutes, until it begins to have a solid texture but doesn't yet form peaks. Stop the mixer and slowly pour in the 3 tablespoons of honey. Stir the mix a few times with a spatula to keep the honey from settling to the bottom.

6   Beat for a few more minutes or until soft peaks form. If you like, you can beat it until you get stiff peaks (it will have a little more texture and a stronger form but might not look as smooth).

7   When the nuts are completely cool, gently remove them from the foil and break the chunks into bite-size pieces.

8   Fill small bowls ⅔ of the way with meadowcream and the remaining ⅓ with nuts.

Enjoy with all your favorite Redwall heroes!

dark chocolate earl grey lavender truffles

from "The Naval Treaty" by Arthur Conan Doyle

Makes 12 truffles

"The table was all laid, and just as I was about to ring Mrs. Hudson entered with the tea and coffee. A few minutes later she brought in three covers, and we all drew up to the table, Holmes ravenous, I curious . . ."
—John Watson

There's nothing more British than Earl Grey tea or Sherlock Holmes, so why not bring them together? These dark chocolate truffles use cream steeped in tea to get that distinct Earl Grey flavor.

INGREDIENTS

1 Earl Grey teabag
¼ cup heavy cream
1 tsp coarsely chopped lavender buds
2 Tbsp cocoa powder
½ bag (5 oz) bittersweet chocolate pieces

Special Tools
Wire mesh strainer
Double boiler

INSTRUCTIONS

1   Remove the tea from the bag and stir it into the cream with the lavender. Cover and let steep 3 hours in the refrigerator.

2   Pour the cocoa powder into a small bowl and set aside. Put the chocolate pieces in the top pan that you will later place over the double boiler. Set aside for the moment.

3   When the cream is almost finished steeping, heat water to boiling in the bottom pan of the double boiler (make sure the water level is low enough that it will not touch the bottom of the top pan when it is placed over the top).

4   Pour the steeped cream into a small saucepan and set the heat to low. Stirring regularly, heat the cream until steaming (about 2 minutes).

5   Turn off the heat from both the saucepan and double boiler. Place the chocolate in the top pan over the boiled water in the double boiler.

6   Pour the cream through a strainer onto the chocolate. Press the lavender buds and tea remnants against the strainer with a spoon to be sure that all excess liquid is removed. Discard the remaining lavender and tea.

7   Allow the cream and chocolate to sit for approximately 3 minutes.

8   Stir until the chocolate is melted and the cream is entirely incorporated into the chocolate. Cover and freeze for 30 minutes in the freezer. Chill in the fridge for 20–30 minutes or until firm all the way to the center.

NOTE: Rolling the chocolate into balls can get messy, but one way to keep your hands a little cleaner is to lay a sheet of plastic wrap over your hand, put the chocolate in your palm, and shape it inside the plastic.

9 Use a spoon to scoop the chocolate out of the bowl and roll it into 1-inch balls. Roll each ball in the cocoa powder. Cover and chill for 5–10 minutes (if the chocolate is difficult to shape into nice round balls, try reshaping them after the chill period).

Top with a sprinkling of lavender buds and serve to your favorite Victorian detective!

delicious death chocolate cake

from *A Murder Is Announced* by Agatha Christie

Makes 1 single-layer 9-inch cake

"Yes. It is rich. For it I have nothing! Impossible to make such a cake. I need for it chocolate and much butter, and sugar and raisins . . . It will be rich, rich, of a melting richness! And on top I will put the icing—chocolate icing . . . Delicious, they will say—delicious."
—Mitzi

This recipe uses gel food coloring instead of liquid coloring to help achieve a strong black color without adding excess water to the frosting.

INGREDIENTS

Frosting
¾ cup whipping cream
¼ cup unsalted butter
⅛ tsp kosher salt
½ bag (6 oz) semisweet
   chocolate chips
40 drops (approximately
   ½ tsp) black
   gel coloring

Cake
¾ cup flour
½ cup unsweetened
   cocoa powder
1 cup sugar
¾ tsp baking soda
½ tsp baking powder
½ tsp salt
1 room temperature egg,
   lightly beaten
½ cup buttermilk
¼ cup melted butter
½ tsp vanilla extract
½ cup hot coffee

Special Tools
Bat stencils
Seasonal silk flowers,
   available in most
   craft stores*

INSTRUCTIONS

1 To make the frosting, heat the cream in a saucepan on medium-low heat until steaming, stirring regularly.

2 Melt the butter in a microwave. Combine all the ingredients in a double boiler over medium-low heat and whisk briskly to combine until completely smooth.

3 Cover and chill for 1 hour. Stir and replace the cover, allow to chill 1½ hours more or until the mix reaches spreading consistency.

4 Preheat your oven to 350°F. Coat a 9-inch round cake pan with cooking spray and line the bottom with a circle of parchment paper. Whisk all the dry ingredients for the cake together in a medium bowl and set aside.

5 Whisk the egg, buttermilk, melted butter, and vanilla together in a large bowl. Gradually whisk the dry mix into the wet mix. Stir in the hot coffee until the mixture is smooth.

Tea pairing
Poirot's Chocolate
Mate Tea, p. 124

* Chrysanthemum blossoms are an edible alternative. If using edible flowers, be sure to use flowers that are clean and free of pesticides and chemicals.

6   Pour the cake batter into the prepared pan. Bake for 25 minutes or until a toothpick inserted in the center comes out clean.

7   Cool the cake in the pan on a wire rack for 10 minutes. Flip the cake out of the pan and allow to cool completely on the rack (approximately 1 hour).

8   Spread the frosting onto the cake in a flat layer. For decoration, lay bat stencils on the frosting and sift powdered sugar over the top, then remove the stencils and add seasonal silk flowers as a topper. Wrap a length of seasonal ribbon around the base of the cake.

Serve at an ill-fated dinner party to unsuspecting guests!

dragon scale madeleines

from *The Hobbit* by J. R. R. Tolkien

Makes 12 madeleines

"There he lay, a vast red-golden dragon, fast asleep . . . Beneath him, under all his limbs and his huge coiled tail, and about him on all sides stretching away across the unseen floors, lay countless piles of precious things, gold wrought and unwrought, gems and jewels, and silver red-stained in the ruddy light."

Madeleines are incredibly versatile. You can experiment with different extracts and food colorings to develop dozens of variations on the classic madeleine. This recipe uses red coloring and gold sprinkles to achieve the look of Smaug's dragon scales.

INGREDIENTS

¼ cup plus 2 Tbsp flour
⅛ tsp baking powder
⅛ tsp salt
1 room temperature egg
½ tsp almond extract
½ cup powdered sugar
¾ tsp red liquid food coloring (or ¼ tsp gel coloring)
¼ cup melted butter, cooled
2 tsp gold sprinkles, divided

Special Tools
Madeleine pan

Tea pairing

Bilbo's Breakfast Brew, p. 120

INSTRUCTIONS

1 Preheat your oven to 375°F. In a small bowl, sift together your flour, baking powder, and salt. Set aside. Lightly coat a madeleine pan with cooking spray and set aside.

2 Beat the egg and almond extract in a standing mixer on high speed for 4 minutes.

3 With the mixer running, beat in the powdered sugar a few tablespoons at a time, stopping to scrape the sides of the bowl if necessary. Add in your food coloring and beat for 5 more minutes.

4 With a spoon or silicone spatula, stir in the flour mix a few tablespoons at a time. Stir in the melted butter in a similar manner. Stir half your sprinkles into the mix.

5 Shake the remaining sprinkles into the molds on the madeleine pan. Scoop a large spoonful of batter into each mold (enough to fill each one about half full).

6 Bake for 6–8 minutes or until the cookies spring back when tapped with a finger. Allow them to cool in the pan on a wire rack for 2–3 minutes. Turn the pan over onto the rack to tip out the cookies. If any cookies stick to the inside of the pan, gently pry them out with the tip of a butter knife.

7 Allow the cookies to cool on the rack for 10–15 minutes.

Serve to a dragon to distract him while you steal his treasure!

NOTE: Madeleines burn quickly, so keep an eye on them for the last few minutes of baking.

Tea pairing

Hundred Acre Tea,
p. 121

eeyore's birthday cake

from *Winnie-the-Pooh* by A. A. Milne

Makes 1 angel food cake

*"You were so busy getting his party ready for him. He had a cake with icing
on the top, and three candles, and his name in pink sugar . . ."*

This lemon angel food cake with blueberry curd filling has all the fun flavors and
whimsical appearance of the finest Hundred Acre dessert.

INGREDIENTS

Blueberry Curd Filling
2 cups blueberries
2 Tbsp lemon juice
1 cup sugar
½ cup butter
2 Tbsp water
2 Tbsp cornstarch

Cake
1 cup flour
1½ cups sugar, divided
1½ cups egg whites,
    room temperature
1½ tsp cream of tartar
1¼ tsp lemon extract
¼ tsp salt

Special Tools
Wire mesh strainer
Tube pan

Decorations (Optional)
Pink icing (store-bought)
Whipped topping
    (store-bought)
Birthday candles
Alphabet cookies (I use
    Trader Joe's Cinnamon
    Schoolbook Cookies)
Pink sugar sprinkles
Fresh blueberries

INSTRUCTIONS

1   To make the curd, heat the blueberries and lemon juice over low heat in a medium saucepan until soft (approximately 5 minutes), stirring occasionally. Strain the mix, pressing the fruit through with a spoon to be sure to get all the juice out, and discard the waste. Return to heat and mix in the sugar and butter until dissolved.

2   Turn the heat to medium and bring the mix to a boil, stirring occasionally.

3   In a small bowl, whisk the water and starch into a slurry. Add the slurry to the blueberry mix and heat 3–4 minutes, stirring continuously. It will thicken slightly.

4   Transfer to a medium bowl and top with plastic wrap, making sure the wrap doesn't touch the hot curd. Allow the curd to cool for 15 minutes on the counter, then chill 2 hours or until completely cool. Chill until ready to use.

5   To make the cake, start by moving the oven rack to the lowest setting and preheating the oven to 350°F. Sift together the flour and ½ cup sugar three times.

6   Add the egg whites, cream of tartar, lemon extract, and salt to the bowl of a standing mixer. Beat on medium speed until soft peaks form (approximately 2–3 minutes).

7   On medium-high speed, beat the remaining 1 cup sugar into the egg mix 1 tablespoon at a time. Continue beating until stiff peaks form (approximately 6–8 minutes).

8   Gradually sift the flour mix into the egg mix ¼ cup at a time, folding to combine after each addition.

* The alphabet cookies should spell "Hipy Bthuthdy" (This is how Owl spells "Happy Birthday" when asked to write it in the book).

9   Pour the mix into an ungreased tube pan. Run a knife in a circle through the middle of the batter to remove any large air bubbles.

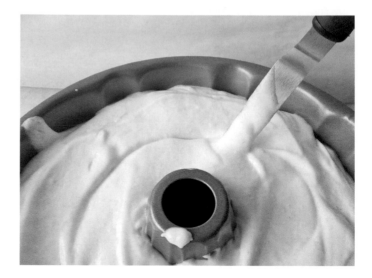

10   Bake 35–45 minutes or until the cake is springy when firmly tapped. Immediately flip the cake pan upside down onto a wire rack, leaving the cake inside. Allow to cool in this manner for 1 hour.

11   Run a knife along the inner and outer edges of the pan to loosen the cake. Quickly flip over onto a serving plate and gently slide off the pan. If desired, you can hold the serving plate in place over the bottom of the pan while flipping for extra security.

12   Cut the cake into two layers and set aside the top layer. Spread blueberry curd over the middle and replace the top layer.

13   To decorate, drizzle the top of the cake with pink icing and scoop on dollops of whipped topping. Stick the candles into the whipped topping. Dip the front of the cookies first in pink icing and then in sugar sprinkles. Clean up any drips with a toothpick. Allow the icing to dry. Arrange the blueberries and cookies around the cake as desired.

Make a wish and serve to your friends in the Hundred Acre Wood!

NOTE: The blueberry curd can be made several days in advance, saving you some time on cake baking day.

fairy dust star cookies

from *Peter Pan* by J. M. Barrie

Makes 20 linzer cookies

"She asked where he lived.
'Second to the right,' said Peter, 'and then straight on till morning.'"

This imaginative take on the linzer cookie features a raspberry jam center and silver sprinkles. Delicately sweet with an otherworldly twinkle, it's a dessert even Tinker Bell couldn't resist.

INGREDIENTS

2 cups flour
½ tsp baking powder
¼ tsp salt
½ cup plus 2 Tbsp butter,
  softened
¾ cup sugar
1 egg, lightly beaten
2 Tbsp milk
2 tsp vanilla extract
¼ cup powdered sugar
¼–½ cup seedless
  raspberry jam
¼ tsp silver sprinkles

Special Tools
3½-inch star
  cookie cutter
2-inch star cookie cutter

Tea pairing

Second Star to the
Right, p. 125

INSTRUCTIONS

1 Whisk together the flour, baking powder, and salt in a bowl and set aside.

2 In a standing mixer, cream together the butter and sugar on medium speed until smooth. Beat in the egg, milk, and vanilla until combined.

3 Gradually beat in the flour mix until just combined, stopping to scrape the sides of the bowl if necessary.

4 Gather the dough together into a ball. Separate into two smaller balls of equal size and wrap tightly in plastic wrap. Freeze for 15 minutes. While waiting, preheat the oven to 325°F. When the 15 minutes are up, unwrap one ball of dough and transfer the other to the fridge.

5 Generously flour a cutting board and rolling pin. Roll out the unwrapped dough to ⅛-inch thickness and cut out 10 stars with a 3½-inch star cookie cutter (if the dough is too stiff to roll, work it with your hands until it is pliable). Place the cookies on an ungreased baking sheet an equal distance apart and bake for 8 minutes. Allow to cool on the pan for 5 minutes before moving to a wire rack to cool completely (if they seem a little stuck to the pan, gently ease them off with a butter knife).

6 Gather your scraps into a ball. Reflour your surface and reroll the dough. Cut out 10 more stars and transfer to a baking sheet. Cut the center out of the stars with a 2-inch star cookie cutter to create hollow stars (discard the center). Bake for 6 minutes. Allow to cool for 5 minutes on the pan before removing to a wire rack to cool completely.

7 Unwrap the second ball of dough and repeat Steps 5 and 6.

8   When the cookies are cool, place the hollow stars on a cutting board and dust powdered sugar through a wire mesh strainer over the cookies until completely coated.

9   Place ½–1 tsp of jam in the middle of each whole star. Place the hollow stars on top, turning them at an angle so that the arms of the bottom star show between the gaps in the arms in the top star. Add a pinch of silver sprinkles to the center of each star.

Serve as an in-flight snack while on your way to Neverland!

hercule poirot's crème de menthe truffles

from *Hickory Dickory Dock* by Agatha Christie

Makes 15 truffles

"We will wish him good luck."
Gravely, Hercule Poirot raised his glass. It contained crème de menthe.
Inspector Sharpe raised his whisky glass.
"Here's hoping," he said.

The Belgian detective Hercule Poirot loves crème de menthe and chocolate, so why not combine them into a luxurious and indulgent Belgian truffle? With just four ingredients, this minty, darkly sweet dessert will set your little gray cells whirring!

INGREDIENTS

½ bag (5 oz) bittersweet chocolate pieces
¼ cup heavy cream
1 Tbsp plus 1 tsp crème de menthe
2–3 Tbsp cocoa powder, for dusting

Special Tools
Double boiler
A sheet of plastic wrap (optional)

Tea pairing

Poirot's Chocolate Mate Tea, p. 124

INSTRUCTIONS

1   Boil water in the bottom of a double boiler. While you wait, heat the cream in a small saucepan on low heat until steaming and just beginning to bubble, stirring regularly. Turn off the heat for both.

2   Add the chocolate to the top of the double boiler. Pour the cream over the top and allow to sit for 3 minutes. Stir until completely incorporated and smooth. Add the crème de menthe and stir again until completely smooth.

3   Transfer to a medium bowl and tightly cover with plastic wrap. Freeze for 1 hour and 15 minutes. Move to the refrigerator and chill for another 10–15 minutes.

4   Scoop and shape the chocolate mix into rough 1 teaspoon balls. The chocolate can be messy, so to keep your hands clean you can use a piece of plastic wrap to shield your hand from the chocolate as you shape the balls.

5   Place them back in the bowl. Cover and chill for 10 more minutes, then refine the shape into smoother balls.

6   Roll in cocoa powder and tap off the excess. Chill in a sealed container until ready to serve.

Serve to Hercule Poirot as a reward for solving a very difficult case!

jo's gingerbread

from *Little Women* by Louisa May Alcott

Makes 30 cookies

"The things were just what I wanted, and all the better for being made instead of bought. Beth's new 'ink bib' was capital, and Hannah's box of hard gingerbread will be a treasure."
—Jo

The instructions here explain how to decorate your gingerbread cookies to look like the four March sisters, but you can also decorate them however you like. If you're feeling ambitious, you can even make other characters from the book: Laurie, Marmie, John Brooke, Professor Bhaer, and even Meg's children!

INGREDIENTS

4 cups flour
1½ tsp baking soda
2¼ tsp ginger
1¼ tsp cinnamon
½ tsp allspice
¾ tsp ground cloves
½ tsp salt
½ cup unsalted butter, softened
¼ cup shortening
½ cup brown sugar
¼ cup granulated sugar
1 egg
¾ cup molasses

Special Tools
3x3½-inch gingerbread woman cookie cutter
Food pen
Icing and sprinkles in various colors

Tea pairing

Jo's Gingerbread Tea, p. 122

INSTRUCTIONS

1 In a medium bowl, stir together the first seven ingredients and set aside.

2 Cream the butter, shortening, and sugars in a standing mixer on medium speed until smooth. Beat in the egg and molasses.

3 Gradually beat in the dry mix until combined, stopping to scrape the bowl if necessary.

4 Gather into a ball and cover with plastic wrap. Chill for 2½ hours or until easy to handle. While you wait, preheat oven to 350°F.

5 Between two sheets of wax paper, roll out half the dough to a little under ¼-inch thickness (wrap the remaining dough in plastic wrap and chill until ready to use). Keeping the paper in place, lay the rolled dough on a baking sheet and chill for 10 minutes. Use a cookie cutter to cut out gingerbread women shapes. If you would like the Meg cookies to have their hair in a bun like the ones shown in the picture, shape small scraps of dough into circles and gently press them on top of the heads of one quarter of the gingerbread women.

6 Place cookies 2 inches apart on a baking sheet lined with parchment paper (if the shapes are too delicate to lift from the paper without tearing, slide an offset spatula or frosting knife underneath to lift them). Bake for 7 minutes or until the edges are set. Allow the cookies to cool for 5 minutes on the baking sheet before moving them to a wire rack to cool completely.

7 Roll, cut out, and bake remaining cookies from second half of dough. Repeat the process with the scraps of dough.

8 Decorate with icing and sprinkles to look like the four March sisters:

- **FOR MEG** Outline and fill the dress using purple icing. Add white pearl sprinkles while the icing is still wet. Draw the face with a food pen and outline the head and the top of the hair bun with chocolate icing.
- **FOR JO** Outline and fill in the dress using white icing, then trace a criss-cross pattern on top with blue icing. Draw the face with a food pen. Make the curls around her head by drawing a loop pattern with chocolate icing. For the braid, draw a zig-zag line one way over her shoulder and draw another zig-zag over it going the opposite way. Finish the braid with a blue icing bow.
- **FOR BETH** Outline and fill the dress using teal icing, then use white icing and some white pearl sprinkles to make a Peter Pan collar with buttons. Draw the face with a food pen. Pipe her hair with chocolate icing by starting below her shoulder, going over her head, and ending below her opposite shoulder. Add a dot of teal icing for a pin in her hair.
- **FOR AMY** Outline and fill the dress using pink icing. Scatter multicolored sprinkles over it before it dries. Draw the face with a food pen. Pipe her hair with yellow icing by starting below her shoulder and piping a zig-zag line over her head and ending below her opposite shoulder. Pipe another line over it, zig-zagging in the opposite direction to give her hair a wavy look. Draw a blue icing bow in her hair.

Serve to a young writer who's just starting out on her own!

Tea pairing

Miss Mary's Garden
Blend, p. 123

lavender lemon eclairs

from *The Secret Garden* by Frances Hodgson Burnett

"At first it seemed that green things would never cease pushing their way through the earth, in the grass, in the beds, even in the crevices of the walls. Then the green things began to show buds and the buds began to unfurl and show color, every shade of blue, every shade of purple, every tint and hue of crimson."

This dessert has three components: choux pastry, pastry cream, and lemon icing. As such, it takes a little extra time to make. However, that doesn't mean you need to spend the whole day in the kitchen. The choux pastry can be made a day in advance, and the pastry cream can be made up to two days in advance.

INGREDIENTS

Pastry Cream
4 cups whole milk
1 Tbsp vanilla extract
1½ Tbsp lavender buds
4 eggs, plus 3 egg yolks
1 cup sugar
6 Tbsp cornstarch
¼ tsp salt

Choux Pastry
½ cup butter
1 cup water
1 cup flour
4 eggs,
    thoroughly beaten

Icing
1 cup powdered sugar
1 Tbsp plus ½ tsp
    lemon juice
4 Tbsp lavender buds

Special Tools
Piping bag fitted with
    ½-inch round tip
Silicone baking mats
    (optional)

INSTRUCTIONS

1   Start by making the pastry cream. Bring the milk, vanilla, and lavender to a boil in a large pot on medium heat, whisking regularly to prevent a skin and an overcooked bottom. As soon as it comes to a boil, turn off the heat. Allow the mix steep for 1 hour uncovered.

2   While the milk steeps, work on the choux pastry. First, move the oven racks to the top and bottom positions. Preheat oven to 400°F. Line two baking sheets with parchment paper or silicone mats and set aside.

3   Melt the butter and water together in a large saucepan on low heat. Turn the heat to medium and bring to a boil. Turn off the heat and pour in the flour all at once. Stir together quickly with a silicone spatula. Turn the heat back to medium. Cook for 2 minutes, stirring constantly. Remove from heat. Beat in the eggs ½ tablespoon at a time with a hand mixer on medium speed until smooth.

4   Fit a piping bag with a ½-inch round tip and fill the bag with the pastry dough.

5   Pipe 12 5-inch eclairs at least 1½ inches apart on each baking sheet. Place the sheets in the oven. Bake for 20 minutes. Turn the heat down to 350°F; flip and rotate the pans. Bake for 20 minutes more. Turn off the heat and let the pastry shells sit for 10 minutes in the oven. Remove to a wire rack to cool.

6   When the milk for the pastry cream has finished steeping, put it on medium heat until it just begins to simmer, whisking regularly to prevent a skin. While you wait, whisk the eggs, yolks, sugar, cornstarch, and salt for the pastry cream together in a bowl. Turn off the heat. Strain the lavender buds out of the heated milk. Very gradually whisk ¼ cup of the heated milk into the egg mix until fully incorporated. Whisk in another ¼ cup the same way. Gradually whisk the tempered egg mix into the rest of the heated milk.

7   Heat on medium, whisking constantly for 3 minutes (the mix will thicken slightly). When it starts to bubble, which should be right after the 3-minute mark, whisk for 1 minute more. Just toward the end, it should thicken considerably.

8   Remove from heat and whisk for another minute or two to get rid of any excess lumps. Cover and chill for 60–90 minutes or until completely cooled.

9   Whisk the cooled pastry cream until smooth. Spoon the pastry cream into a piping bag with a ½-inch round tip. Cut the pastry shells in half lengthwise and fill with cream.

10   To make the icing, whisk the powdered sugar and lemon juice together. Drizzle on the icing with a spoon and sprinkle the lavender buds on top.

Serve at a garden party at a grand English manor!

NOTE: While steeping, the pastry cream may develop a skin, and that's fine. Just whisk it in when you start working with the cream again. You just don't want a skin to develop while the mix is cooking, since it can trap heat and cause the mix to overcook.

lemon turkish delight

from *The Lion, the Witch, and the Wardrobe* by C. S. Lewis

Makes 32 pieces

"The Queen let another drop fall from her bottle on to the snow, and instantly there appeared a round box, tied with green silk ribbon, which, when opened, turned out to contain several pounds of the best Turkish Delight. Each piece was sweet and light to the very centre and Edmund had never tasted anything more delicious."

Turkish delight is a dish than fascinates many, but its traditional flavor combinations (like rose and pistachio) can be daunting to people trying it for the first time. This recipe has a simple lemon flavor, making it more accessible to those who are new to it. Many Turkish delight recipes are also quite complicated, requiring hours of simmering and special tools like candy thermometers. This recipe, however, is Turkish Delight made easy! The key lies in allowing the gelatin to simmer with the sugar mix, instead of adding it later. The result is a simple, forgiving recipe with few ingredients, and the final product is sweet, gummy, and very soft—a delicious introduction to the food of Narnia!

INGREDIENTS

2 cups sugar
¾ cup cold water
2 packets gelatin (a little under 1½ Tbsp)
1½ tsp fresh lemon juice
2 tsp lemon extract
2 drops yellow food coloring
½ cup powdered sugar
½ cup cornstarch

INSTRUCTIONS

1 Very generously spray and flour a 10x5-inch metal loaf pan and set aside. Gently stir the sugar, cold water, and gelatin in a medium saucepan until combined. Heat the mix on medium heat until the sugar dissolves, stirring regularly. Bring the mix to a boil, and then immediately turn the heat down to low (keep a close eye on it—the mix will start to foam upward quickly when it starts to boil and could overflow if allowed to continue). Simmer for 10 minutes without stirring. The mixture will be very foamy.

2 Remove from heat. Quickly stir in the lemon juice, lemon extract, and food coloring. *Be careful, as the sugar mix is very hot and will foam upward slightly.*

3 Quickly pour the mix into the prepared pan and chill for 4–6 hours.

4 Whisk the powdered sugar and cornstarch in a medium bowl. Sprinkle a generous layer of the sugar-cornstarch mix onto a cutting board. Loosen the candy mix from the edges of the pan with a sharp knife coated with cooking spray. Overturn the candy onto the cutting board (you may need to ease it from the bottom of the pan with the knife before overturning). Cut the mix into squares approximately 1 inch across, respraying the knife if it starts to stick. Very gently toss the pieces in the powdered sugar mix to coat.

5   These can be eaten right away. The pieces can also be allowed to set overnight on a shallow bed of the sugar-cornstarch mix in a large, lightly covered dish with tall sides (like a glass baking dish). Overnight setting will achieve a slightly more stable consistency.

Serve to any Sons of Adam or Daughters of Eve you find wandering through Narnia's winter woodland!

long john's lime cookies

from *Treasure Island* by Robert Louis Stevenson

Makes 20 cookies

"And thereupon we all entered the cave . . . and in a far corner, only duskily flickered over by the blaze, I beheld great heaps of coin and quadrilaterals built of bars of gold. That was Flint's treasure that we had come so far to seek."

These lime cookies are the perfect Treasure Island dessert—crisp and light with just a hint of lime and sweet powdered sugar. They're just the thing to cheer you up when you and your pirate buddies have lost your treasure to that meddling cabin boy!

INGREDIENTS

½ cup butter, softened
2 Tbsp granulated sugar
¼ cup powdered sugar
¼ tsp salt
1 tsp grated lime peel
2 tsp lime juice
1 cup flour
⅛ tsp baking powder
Extra grated lime peel,
    for garnish
Extra powdered sugar
    (about ½ cup),
    for garnish

Tea pairing

Long John's Island
Blend, p. 122

INSTRUCTIONS

1   In an electric mixer on medium-high speed, cream the butter, granulated sugar, ¼ cup powdered sugar, salt, and lime peel until smooth. If necessary, stop halfway through to scrape the sides of the bowl. With the mixer running, add the lime juice and beat until combined. Gradually beat in the flour and baking powder, stopping to scrape if necessary.

2   Shape the dough into a 9-inch log and wrap the log in plastic wrap. Freeze for 25 minutes. Preheat oven to 400°F.

3   Slice the log into disks that are a little under ½-inch thick.

4   Place 12 of the disks 2 inches apart on an ungreased baking sheet and bake for 8–10 minutes or until the cookies are set and have just a touch of brown around the edges. While the first batch bakes, rewrap the remainder of the log in plastic wrap and chill until ready to begin the second batch.

5   Allow the finished cookies to cool for 5 minutes on the baking sheet. Transfer to a wire rack to cool completely.

6   Bake and cool the remaining disks.

7   Place your extra powdered sugar in a bowl. Gently toss the cookies in the powdered sugar and top with extra grated lime peel.

Enjoy while hunting for Captain Flint's treasure!

peppermint humbugs

from *A Christmas Carol* by Charles Dickens

Makes approximately 20 candies

"'A merry Christmas, uncle! God save you!' cried a cheerful voice. It was the voice of Scrooge's nephew, who came upon him so quickly that this was the first intimation he had of his approach.
'Bah!' said Scrooge, 'Humbug!'"

Humbugs are traditional British mint hard candies often served at Christmas. This recipe is unique in that each of the pieces has a fun, one-of-a-kind shape, which comes from twisting the candy before it sets. Using regular mint extract instead of peppermint gives them a lightly minted, almost creamy flavor.

INGREDIENTS

½ cup sugar
3 Tbsp corn syrup
2½ Tbsp water
¼ tsp fresh lemon juice
½ tsp mint extract
3 drops pastel green
   gel coloring

Special Tools
Candy thermometer
Clean, unused
   rubber gloves
Kitchen scissors

INSTRUCTIONS

1   Liberally coat a bread pan with cooking spray and set aside.

2   In a medium saucepan, combine the sugar, corn syrup, water, and lemon juice. Stirring constantly, cook on medium-high heat until the sugar dissolves and the mix begins to boil.

3   Reduce the heat to medium and insert a candy thermometer. Allow the mix to heat until it reaches 300°F, stirring occasionally.

4   Turn off the heat and quickly stir in the extract and food coloring. Pour the mix into the prepared pan. Allow the mix to rest for 4–4½ minutes.

5   Put on clean, unused rubber gloves and liberally coat the hands of the gloves with cooking spray. Pick up the candy mix and work it into a rope shape by pulling, twisting, and folding it over itself. (It will be very hot, but it will be easier to work with if you work quickly. If it's still too hot to hold for even a few seconds, allow it to rest for 30 more seconds in the pan. After a time, the candy may be cool enough for you to take off your gloves.)

6 When the candy starts to get too stiff to work with, roll it into a rope and lay it on a sheet of wax paper. Moving down the rope an inch or so at a time, twist it until the entire length of the rope is a tight corkscrew.

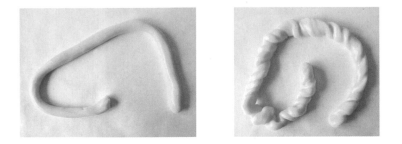

7 Cut the rope into bite-size pieces with kitchen scissors coated with cooking spray. Allow the pieces to set on the wax paper for 30 minutes or until completely cool and hard.

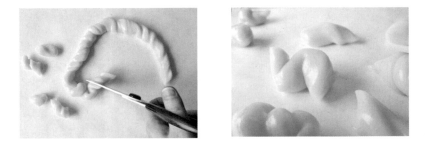

8 Wrap the candies in small squares of wax paper and twist the ends to secure.

Serve to Ebenezer Scrooge to lift his spirits!

Tea pairing

Drink Me Tea, p. 121

queen of hearts' painted rose cupcakes

from *Alice's Adventures in Wonderland* by Lewis Carroll

Makes 12 cupcakes

"A large rose-tree stood near the entrance of the garden: the roses growing on it were white, but there were three gardeners at it, busily painting them red. Alice thought this a very curious thing . . ."

Chocolate cake, cherry filling, and two-toned buttercream roses—what's not to love? These white rose cupcakes get their distinctive red streaks from intermittent drops of gel coloring added between scoops of frosting in the piping bag before decorating.

INGREDIENTS

Cake
½ cup flour
½ cup cocoa powder
½ tsp baking powder
¼ tsp baking soda
¼ tsp salt
¼ cup butter, softened
¾ cups sugar
1 tsp vanilla extract
2 eggs,
  room temperature
2½ Tbsp sour cream
¾ tsp distilled
  white vinegar
½ cup buttermilk,
  room temperature
¼ cup plus 2 Tbsp
  cherry preserves

Frosting
¾ cup butter, softened
3 cups powdered sugar
3 Tbsp milk
1½ tsp vanilla extract
Approximately 8–10
  drops red gel coloring

Special Tools
Melon baller
Piping bag fitted with a
  large star tip

INSTRUCTIONS

1 Preheat oven to 350°F. Fill a cupcake tin with liners and set it aside. In a medium bowl, whisk together all the dry ingredients except the sugar. Set aside.

2 In a large bowl, cream the butter on medium speed with a hand mixer. Beat in the sugar and vanilla until combined. Beat in the eggs 1 at a time. Beat in the sour cream and vinegar. Alternate beating in the dry mix and buttermilk.

3 Fill the cupcake liners half full and bake for 15–17 minutes or until a toothpick inserted in the center comes out clean. Set the cupcakes on a wire rack to cool.

4 When the cupcakes are cool, scoop ½ tablespoon of cake from the center of each cupcake with a melon baller. Fill the hole in each cupcake with cherry preserves.

5 To make the frosting, sift the powdered sugar in a medium bowl and set aside. Beat the butter in a standing mixer on medium speed until smooth. Beat in 1 cup powdered sugar until fluffy. Beat in the vanilla extract and 1 tablespoon of milk. Alternate beating in the remaining powdered sugar and milk.

6 In a piping bag fitted with a large star tip, add 1 large spoonful of frosting. Add 2 drops of coloring. Scoop in 2 large spoonfuls of frosting and add 2 more drops of coloring. Continue alternating frosting and coloring until the bag is full. Squish the bag in several spots to distribute the coloring in swirls. Pipe roses by starting in the center of each cupcake and circling outward in a spiral motion.

Serve after a long afternoon of painting the roses red!

Tea pairing

Lovers' Tea, p. 123

romeo's sighs and juliet's kisses

from *Romeo and Juliet* by William Shakespeare

Makes 22 sandwich cookies

*"I dreamt my lady came and found me dead–
Strange dream, that gives a dead man leave to think!–
And breathed such life with kisses in my lips,
That I revived, and was an emperor."*
—Act V, Scene 1

In modern day Verona, toasted almond and chocolate sandwich cookies, referred to as Sospri di Romeo and Baci di Giulietta ("Romeos Sighs" and "Juliet's Kisses"), are sold in pastry shops in honor of the Shakespearean characters. Traditionally, the dessert is sold in mixed bags of almond cookies and chocolate cookies, but I like how some bakers combine both types into one sandwich cookie, as I have here.

INGREDIENTS

Romeo Cookies
½ cup butter, softened
¼ cup powdered sugar
¼ cup granulated sugar
¼ tsp salt
¾ tsp almond extract
2 Tbsp milk
1 cup flour
⅛ tsp baking powder

Juliet Cookies
¾ cup flour
¼ cup cocoa powder
⅛ tsp baking powder
½ cup butter, softened
¼ cup powdered sugar
¼ cup granulated sugar
¼ tsp salt
1 tsp vanilla extract
2 Tbsp milk
¼ cup toasted almonds,
    finely crushed

Filling
½ cup bittersweet
    chocolate pieces
2 Tbsp butter
½ cup toasted almonds,
    finely crushed

Special Tools
Double boiler

INSTRUCTIONS

1   To make the Romeo cookies, cream the butter, sugars, and salt in the bowl of a standing mixer until smooth. With the beater running, add the almond extract and milk, scraping the sides of the bowl if necessary. Gradually beat in the flour and baking powder. Roll the mix into a 9-inch log and wrap in plastic wrap. Set aside.

2   To make the Juliet cookies, stir together the flour, cocoa powder, and baking powder in a small bowl. Set aside. In the bowl of a standing mixer, cream together the butter, sugars, and salt until smooth. With the beater running, beat in the vanilla and milk. Gradually beat in the flour mix. Stir in the crushed almonds. Roll the mix into a 9-inch log and wrap in plastic wrap.

3   Freeze the two logs for 25 minutes. Preheat oven to 400°F.

4   Remove the wrapping from the almond dough and place the chocolate dough in the refrigerator. Slice the almond dough into disks a little under ½-inch thick and bake for 8 minutes on a baking sheet lined with parchment paper. Allow the cookies to cool for 5 minutes on the baking sheet before transferring to a wire rack to cool completely. Repeat this process with the chocolate dough.

5   To make the filling, melt the chocolate pieces and butter over a double boiler, stirring until smooth. Stir in the almonds.

6 Flip all your chocolate cookies so that they are bottom side up. Spread approximately ½ teaspoon of filling onto each chocolate cookie. Gently press the white cookies on top.

Serve as a travel snack to the love of your life while touring the streets of Verona!

sara crewe's rose cake

from *A Little Princess* by Frances Hodgson Burnett

Makes 12 cupcakes or 6 mini layer cakes

"Sara opened a cupboard and gave her a thick slice of cake . . . Becky was almost speechless with admiration. Then she said in an awed voice, 'Once I see a princess . . . She was a growed-up young lady, but she was pink all over—gownd an' cloak, an' flowers an' all. I called her to mind the minnit I see you, sittin' there on the table, miss. You looked like her.'"

I love the friendship that develops between Becky and Sara in *A Little Princess*. At first, Becky the maid is shy and uncertain around Sara, and Sara is lonely in an unfamiliar country. But when Sara sees how hungry Becky is, she shares all kinds of food with her, starting with this cake (which I modeled after the rosy dress Becky says she once saw on a real princess). Becky is touched by the generosity and soon gets over her shyness, opening the door for a friendship that both girls desperately need.

INGREDIENTS

Cake
1 cup flour
½ tsp baking powder
¼ tsp baking soda
¼ tsp salt
¼ cup butter, softened
¾ cups sugar
1 tsp vanilla extract
2 egg whites,
    room temperature
2½ Tbsp sour cream
¾ tsp distilled
    white vinegar
½ cup buttermilk,
    room temperature

Frosting
3 cups powdered sugar
¾ cup butter, softened
1½ tsp raspberry extract
3 Tbsp milk
Pink food coloring

Decoration
White icing roses and daisies (the amount you need will be determined by their size)
White pearl sprinkles, enough to place 3 between each icing rose
Silk flowers, for topper

INSTRUCTIONS

1 Preheat oven to 350°F. Fill a cupcake tin with liners and set it aside.

2 To prepare the cake, whisk together the all dry ingredients except the sugar in a medium bowl. Set aside.

3 In a large bowl, cream the butter on medium speed with a hand mixer. Beat in the sugar and vanilla until combined. Beat in the egg whites one at a time. Beat in the sour cream and vinegar. Alternate beating in the dry mix and buttermilk.

4 Fill the cupcake liners half full and bake for 15 minutes or until a toothpick inserted in the center comes out clean. Set the cupcakes on a wire rack. When they are completely cool, remove the liners.

5 To make the frosting, sift the powdered sugar in a medium bowl and set aside. Beat the butter in a standing mixer on medium speed until smooth. Beat in 1 cup of powdered sugar until fluffy. Beat in the raspberry extract and 1 tablespoon of milk. Alternate beating in the remaining powdered sugar and milk. Beat in pink food coloring until the desired shade of pink is reached.

6　Level the tops of your cupcakes. Turn half the cupcakes upside down and apply a layer of frosting to what is now the top of the cupcakes. Turn the other half upside down and place them on top of the frosted cupcakes. You will now have 6 mini layer cakes.

7　Frost the outside of your cakes. The cake pictured features decorative vertical lines that can be achieved by moving an icing knife in vertical strokes across the sides of the cake after frosting has been applied and smoothed in a flat layer. Any type of decorative frosting technique is suitable, but a simple technique is recommended so as not to distract from the decorations.

8　Place the icing daisies in a ring around the top of each cake. Alternate placing icing roses and groups of 3 sprinkles around the base of each cake. Top with silk flowers.

Serve to a new friend!

tom sawyer's whitewashed mini jelly doughnuts

from *The Adventures of Tom Sawyer* by Mark Twain

Makes 48 mini doughnuts

"Why, ain't that work?"
Tom resumed his whitewashing, and answered carelessly:
"Well, maybe it is, and maybe it ain't. All I know, is, it suits Tom Sawyer."

The first time we meet our titular character, he's caught stealing jelly from his aunt's pantry. Later, he's conning his friends into white-washing his fence for him. The combo of these incidents got me thinking about jelly doughnuts with a dusting of powdered sugar on top. After all, when it comes to doughnuts, any excuse is a good excuse!

INGREDIENTS

1 packet (7 grams) active
   dry yeast
2½ Tbsp sugar
⅔ cup lukewarm milk
6 Tbsp unsalted butter
3½ cups flour
1 cup sour cream
1 egg
¼ tsp kosher salt
½ tsp cinnamon
¼ tsp almond extract
vegetable oil for frying
6 oz seedless
   raspberry jam
¼ cup powdered sugar,
   for dusting

Special Tools
2-inch round
   cookie cutter

Tea pairing

Becky's White Peach
Tea, p. 119

INSTRUCTIONS

1   Gently mix the yeast, sugar, and milk in a small bowl. Let sit for 15 minutes.

2   Melt the butter in the microwave. In the bowl of a standing mixer fitted with a paddle attachment, beat together the butter, flour, sour cream, egg, salt, cinnamon, almond extract, and yeast mix on medium-low speed until combined (1–2 minutes).

3   Lightly coat a large bowl with cooking spray. Place the dough inside and lightly cover with a clean kitchen towel. Let the dough rest in a warm place for 1–2 hours.

4   Fill the bottom 3–4 inches of a large pot with vegetable oil. Place over medium heat until it sizzles strongly when a bit of dough is flicked in.

5   As the oil heats, roll out half the dough to ½-inch thickness on a floured surface. Cut out circles with a 2-inch round cookie cutter.

6   Repeat Step 5 with the remaining half of dough. Wad up the scraps, reroll, and cut out more circles.

7   Fry the circles for 1–2 minutes on each side until golden. Set the finished doughnuts on a wire rack placed over a baking sheet.

8   Fill a piping bag with jam. Cut slits in the doughnuts and fill with jam. Dust the tops with powdered sugar.

Serve as a reward to the hardworking kids who just painted your fence!

homemade
tea blends

Have you ever wondered how teamakers come up with those delicious, complex-tasting tea blends? It's actually quite simple, and you can even do it in your own kitchen. Just start with a few basic tea flavors and mix different proportions of them together until you get just the right balance.

When designing teas based on books, I like to take my inspiration from something iconic in the story. It might be a character like Becky from *Tom Sawyer* or the guiding star from *Peter Pan*. Then I try to imagine what sorts of flavors would evoke the right ideas. It takes some experimentation to perfect it sometimes, but that's part of the fun!

a note about tea

A "good cup of tea" is very much a matter of personal taste. As such, any instructions regarding amount of tea leaves, water temperature, and additions like sugar aren't strict rules. Think of them more as a place to start.

I like my black teas strong with sugar and milk, but I prefer my green and herbal teas in the form of sun tea sweetened with honey. However, you may find that your tastes are completely different.

Just remember—there are no wrong answers. Whatever tastes good to you is the right way to make tea!

BREWING INSTRUCTIONS

For Black/Chai/Lapsang Souchong/Mate Tea: In this cookbook, all teas in these varieties are designed to be brewed hot. Steep 1–2 teaspoon of the leaves for 3–5 minutes in hot water from a tea kettle. Add sugar and milk as desired. Each blend makes 3–6 mugs of tea.

For Green/Herbal/Oolong/White Tea: In this cookbook, all teas in these varieties are designed to be sun teas. Steep the leaves in 8 cups cold water in a sealed, transparent pitcher for 4 hours (place the pitcher in the sun if possible). Add sugar or honey as desired. Each blend makes 8 cups of tea.

It should be noted that that mentions of "vanilla" and "cream" refer to teas of that flavor, not extracts or dairy. If a blend includes multiple varieties of tea, it is labeled as whatever tea makes up the majority (the teas that appear in the blend in a lesser concentration have their varieties listed for clarification).

abbot's chocolate hazelnut tea

from the Redwall series by Brian Jacques

BLACK

After a long trek through Mossflower Woods, this chocolate hazelnut blend with just a hint of cream is the perfect cozy conclusion to a day at Redwall Abbey.

2 tsp chocolate
2 tsp honeybush
1 tsp hazelnut
1 tsp cream

FOOD PAIRING: Candied Nuts with Meadowcream (p. 77)

arrietty's cherry tree tea

from *The Borrowers* by Mary Norton

GREEN

Inspired by the blossoming cherry tree Arrietty sees on her first day Borrowing with her father, this sweet summery blend will take you right into her world.

4 tsp cherry
2 tsp raspberry

FOOD PAIRING: Badger's Set Salad Bites (p. 15), Arrietty's Mini Cherry Cakes (p. 69)

becky's white peach tea

from *The Adventures of Tom Sawyer* by Mark Twain

WHITE

A light, gently sweet blend of fresh peaches and sun-ripened strawberries, the perfect refreshment after some summer adventuring with Tom Sawyer.

3½ tsp peach
2½ tsp strawberry

FOOD PAIRING: Tom Sawyer's Whitewashed Mini Jelly Doughnuts (p. 115)

bilbo's breakfast brew

from *The Hobbit* by J. R. R. Tolkien

BLACK

A cozy blend of English Breakfast, nuts, and cream to sip while dining in your hobbit hole.

3 tsp chestnut
2 tsp English Breakfast
1 tsp cream

FOOD PAIRING: Beorn's Honey Nut Banana Bread (p. 53), Dragon Scale Madeleines (p. 85)

christmas tea with scrooge

from *A Christmas Carol* by Charles Dickens

BLACK

This festive blend of chestnut and gingerbread will warm you right down to your toes on a Christmas Eve night.

3 tsp chestnut
3 tsp gingerbread

deduction: a sherlock tea

from the Sherlock Holmes series by Arthur Conan Doyle

TOASTED MATE

Toasted mate tea with hazelnut and a hint of smoke, a robust blend reminiscent of the streets of Victorian London.

3 tsp toasted mate
2 tsp hazelnut (black)
1 tsp lapsang souchong

FOOD PAIRING: Sherlock's Steak Sandwiches (p. 45), Blood Orange Scones (p. 57)

drink me tea

from *Alice's Adventures in Wonderland* by Lewis Carroll

WHITE

Delicate white peony tea with just a touch of fruitiness. A perfect refreshment after an afternoon of painting the roses red!

4 tsp peony
2 tsp pear

FOOD PAIRING: Bread and Butterflies (p. 19), Queen of Hearts' Painted Rose Cupcakes (p. 107)

emerald city tea

from *The Wonderful Wizard of Oz* by L. Frank Baum

HERBAL

Click your heels three times and wish for another cup of this mint and lemon blend.

2½ tsp peppermint
1¾ tsp spearmint
1¾ tsp lemon grass

FOOD PAIRING: Cyclone Cookies (p. 73)

hundred acre tea

from *Winnie-the-Pooh* by A. A. Milne

BLACK

This cozy tea features sweet honeybush and toasty hazelnut flavors, with just a touch of cream. The perfect afternoon smackerel to share with your favorite bear!

2½ tsp hazelnut
2½ tsp honeybush
½ tsp vanilla
½ tsp cream

FOOD PAIRING: Haycorns for Piglet (p. 31), Eeyore's Birthday Cake (p. 87)

jo's gingerbread tea

from *Little Women* by Louisa May Alcott

BLACK

Toast a beloved literary heroine with a sweet spiced tea reminiscent of gingerbread cookies.

3 tsp gingerbread
2 tsp ginger
1 tsp cream

FOOD PAIRING: Hannah's Muffs (p. 29), Jo's Gingerbread (p. 94)

lone wolf tea

from *White Fang* by Jack London

LAPSANG SOUCHONG

A smoky tea lightened with honeybush, vanilla, and cream that calls to mind campfires and mountain trails.

1½ tsp lapsang souchong
1½ tsp honeybush
1½ tsp vanilla (black)
1½ tsp cream (black)

FOOD PAIRING: Arctic Trial Coffee Muffins (p. 51)

long john's island blend

from *Treasure Island* by Robert Louis Stevenson

HERBAL

This airy, tropical blend gives you a glimpse of island life without ever having to leave home . . . much like the book!

3½ tsp piña colada tea
2½ tsp mango tea

FOOD PAIRING: Long John's Lime Cookies (p. 103)

lovers' tea

from *Romeo and Juliet* by William Shakespeare

BLACK

The classic romantic flavor of chocolate-dipped strawberries in the form of tea.

3 tsp chocolate
2½ tsp strawberry
½ tsp cream

FOOD PAIRING: Romeo's Sighs and Juliet's Kisses (p. 109)

masquerade tea

from *The Phantom of the Opera* by Gaston Leroux

BLACK

Lose yourself in the rich, dark flavor of chocolate and raspberry.

3 tsp chocolate
2½ tsp raspberry
½ tsp cream

FOOD PAIRING: Devils on Horseback: Bacon Wrapped Dates (p. 27)

miss mary's garden blend

from *The Secret Garden* by Frances Hodgson Burnett

BLACK

Misselthwaite Manor's best kept secret! This tea combines Earl Grey, sweet rose tea, and a touch of strawberry flavor for the experience of a summer garden right in your teacup.

3 tsp Earl Grey
1¼ tsp rose
1¼ tsp strawberry
½ tsp lavender buds

FOOD PAIRING: Candied Flower Cookies (p. 71), Lavender Lemon Eclairs (p. 97)

once and future tea

from *The Story of King Arthur and His Knights* by Howard Pyle

WHITE

Inspired by the misty island of Avalon, this light, ethereal blend features fresh floral and fruit flavors. Sip while you wait for the Once and Future King to rise from his ancient sleep.

4 tsp peony
2 tsp blueberry

poirot's chocolate mate tea

from the Hercule Poirot mystery series by Agatha Christie

TOASTED MATE

Hercule Poirot's famous love for chocolate inspired this toasted nut and chocolate tea. It's just the right blend to sip while reading an intriguing murder mystery.

3 tsp toasted mate
2 tsp chocolate (black)
1 tsp hazelnut (black)

FOOD PAIRING: Miss Marple's "Pocket Full of Rye" Tea Sandwiches (p. 32), Delicious Death Chocolate Cake (p. 81), Hercule Poirot's Crème de Menthe Truffles (p. 93)

princess sara's chocolate chai

from *A Little Princess* by Frances Hodgson Burnett

CHAI

Sip this spiced chocolate and masala chai blend while listening to Sara Crewe tell one of her amazing tales of life in India.

2 tsp masala chai
2 tsp chocolate (black)
1 tsp vanilla (black)
½ tsp cinnamon (black)
½ tsp whole cloves

FOOD PAIRING: Blackberry Lemon Sweet Rolls (p. 55)

quoth the raven

from "The Raven" by Edgar Allan Poe

BLACK

Earl Grey combines with blackberry and cream to make the perfect companion to your midnight musings.

3½ tsp Earl Grey
1½ tsp blackberry
½ tsp cream
½ tsp vanilla

raspberry cordial tea

from *Anne of Green Gables* by L. M. Montgomery

BLACK

Inspired by one of Anne Shirley's favorite beverages, this blend brings Green Gables to life in a teacup.

3½ tsp raspberry
2½ tsp cherry

FOOD PAIRING: Poetical Egg Salad Sandwiches (p. 41)

second star to the right

from *Peter Pan* by J. M. Barrie

BLACK

A soothing blend guaranteed to make you dream of Neverland.

3¾ tsp Earl Grey
1 tsp vanilla
1 tsp cream
¼ tsp lavender buds

FOOD PAIRING: Fairy Dust Star Cookies (p. 89)

summery peach tea

from *James and the Giant Peach* by Roald Dahl

OOLONG

Prepare a cup as you fly your giant peach from England all the way to New York City.

3½ tsp peach oolong
2½ tsp apricot (green)

FOOD PAIRING: Big Apple Hand Pies (p. 17)

tea with tumnus

from the Chronicles of Narnia by C. S. Lewis

BLACK

Settle in with this cozy cranberry almond blend as you listen to tales of Narnia's Long Winter.

3 tsp cranberry
2 tsp almond
1 tsp chocolate

FOOD PAIRING: Apple of Life Bites (p. 13)

tea alternatives

If tea isn't your favorite thing, there are still lots of fun alternatives you can serve at teatime. Hot chocolate is an abiding favorite, but you can also serve cider, punch, coffee, and more. Even if you *do* enjoy tea, it can be nice to try something new—like tea lattes!

Remember, the important thing about teatime is to relax and enjoy delicious food with tasty beverages. So whatever helps you do that is fair game!

autumn harvest cider

from *Triss: A Tale of Redwall* by Brian Jacques

Makes 6 cups hot cider

"Cider was the main drink, but that also had a lot of different varieties: cider with damson, plum' n' apple cider, dandelion burdock cidermix, to name but a few. Then two empty barrels were rolled out and used as drums, a hogwife played a rustic melody on a reed flute and a stout farmer sang out in a fine tenor voice ..."

This seasonal take on classic cider combines sweet-tart apples with the flavors of butterscotch and pumpkin pie.

INGREDIENTS

6 Fuji apples
2 Granny Smith apples
2 oranges, peeled
2 cinnamon sticks,
    snapped in half
4 tsp pumpkin pie spice
1½ tsp whole cloves
7 cups water
⅔ cup butterscotch sauce

Special Tools
Slow cooker
Wire mesh strainer

INSTRUCTIONS

1 Cut the apples into eighths and the oranges into quarters. Cut the seeded portions from the apples and discard.

2 Add everything except the butterscotch sauce to a slow cooker. Cook on high for 5 hours or until the apples are very soft.

3 Strain the liquid. You can transfer it to a pitcher or punch bowl or pour it back in the slow cooker set on warm. Stir in the butterscotch sauce until dissolved.

Serve warm to the good beasts of Redwall during a fine feast!

hundred acre hot chocolate

from *The House at Pooh Corner* by A. A. Milne

Makes 5 cups hot chocolate

"The wind was against them now, and Piglet's ears streamed behind him like banners as he fought his way along, and it seemed hours before he got them into the shelter of the Hundred Acre Wood . . ."

This cinnamon caramel hot chocolate will warm you right down to your toes—the perfect smackerel for a blustery day!

INGREDIENTS

⅓ cup cocoa powder
½–1 tsp instant coffee
1 tsp cinnamon
½ tsp vanilla extract
¾ cup caramel sauce
2 cups half and half
2 cups milk
Whipped cream and extra cinnamon (optional)

INSTRUCTIONS

1 In a medium saucepan, whisk together the first 5 ingredients until the cocoa powder has fully incorporated into the caramel, giving you a thick, sticky paste.

2 Gradually whisk in the dairy until the mixture is smooth. Drag a spatula across the bottom and corners of the pan to make sure the caramel mix has fully incorporated.

3 Place the pan on medium heat for 6–8 minutes or until the hot chocolate is steaming, whisking once every minute or so.

4 Top with whipped cream and a dash of cinnamon.

Serve to Pooh and friends on a chilly autumn day!

london fog lattes

from "The Adventure of the Copper Beeches" by Arthur Conan Doyle

Makes 5 cups "latte tea"

"It was a cold morning of the early spring, and we sat after breakfast on either side of a cheery fire in the old room at Baker Street. A thick fog rolled down between the lines of dun-coloured houses, and the opposing windows loomed like dark, shapeless blurs through the heavy yellow wreaths . . ."

These Earl Grey lattes are lightly sweetened with honey and feature thick, velvety foam.

INGREDIENTS

1 cup milk
4 Earl Grey tea bags
1 tsp coconut extract
¼ cup honey

INSTRUCTIONS

1 Brew the teabags for 7 minutes in 4 cups of very hot water from a tea kettle. While you wait, heat the milk in a saucepan on low heat, stirring regularly.

2 Add the tea, extract, and honey to a blender. Gradually add half the milk and blend for 1 minute. Add the remaining milk and blend for 1 minute more.

Serve on a mysterious, foggy day in London!

« XVI »

...NA IS INVITED TO TEA
...WITH TRAGIC RESULTS

...EAUTIFUL MONTH AT GREEN GABLES, WI...
...hollow turned as golden as sunshine a...
...d the orchard were royal crimson and t...
...along the lane put on the loveliest shades...
...green, while the fields sunned themselve...

...the world of colour about her.
...he exclaimed one Saturday morning, coming...
...arms full of gorgeous boughs, "I'm so glad...
...here there are Octobers. It would be terrible if...
...m September to November, wouldn't it? Look...
...ranches. Don't they give you a thrill—several...
...to decorate my room with them."
...s," said Marilla, whose aesthetic sense was not...
...loped. "You clutter up your room entirely too...
...t-doors stuff, Anne. Bedrooms were made to...

raspberry cordial

from *Anne of Green Gables* by L. M. Montgomery

Makes 4 cups raspberry cordial

"When Anne came back from the kitchen Diana was drinking her second glassful of cordial; and, being entreated thereto by Anne, she offered no particular objection to the drinking of a third. The tumblerfuls were generous ones and the raspberry cordial was certainly very nice."

If you're curious about what Anne Shirley's raspberry cordial tasted like, now you can easily make your own! Swapping out different fruit is a cinch, so you can experiment with lots of different flavored cordials as well.

INGREDIENTS

4 cups fresh raspberries
1 cup sugar
2½ cups water

Special Tools
Wire mesh strainer

NOTE: To make Raspberry Cordial Punch, mix the finished cordial with 4 cups chilled ginger ale and 2 cups chilled white grape juice.

INSTRUCTIONS

1   Combine the ingredients in a medium saucepan on high heat. Stir until the sugar is dissolved. Bring the mix to a boil. Turn the heat to low and allow the mix to simmer for 5 minutes, stirring regularly, until the fruit is soft and mostly separated.

2   Turn off the heat and coarsely mash the mixture to separate the remaining fruit. Strain the mix through a wire mesh strainer into a large mason jar or pitcher with a lid, making sure to press the seeds in the strainer with a spoon several times to get all the juice out.

3   Seal the pitcher and chill for 1–2 hours or until completely cold.

Serve to your best friend during an afternoon visit!

white witch hot chocolate

from *The Lion, the Witch, and the Wardrobe* by C. S. Lewis

Makes a little under 5 cups hot chocolate

*"The Queen took from somewhere among her wrappings a very small bottle . . .
She let one drop fall from it on the snow beside the sledge. Edmund saw the drop for
a second in mid-air, shining like a diamond. But the moment it touched the snow there
was a hissing sound and there stood a jewelled cup full of something that steamed . . .
It was something he had never tasted before, very sweet and foamy and creamy,
and it warmed him right down to his toes."*

This white hot chocolate is flavored with almond extract and a bit of white rum—sure to
keep you warm during the long Narnian winter!

INGREDIENTS

4 cups milk
**1 cup white
chocolate chips**
½ tsp almond extract
2 pinches of salt
**¼ cup white rum
(optional)**

INSTRUCTIONS

1 Combine all the ingredients except the rum in a
saucepan over medium-low heat.

2 Whisk until the chocolate is dissolved. Heat until the
milk is steaming, whisking regularly to keep the chocolate
from forming a layer on the bottom.

3 Remove from heat and whisk in the rum.

Serve in a sledge during the long Narnian winter!

conversion table

Ingredient	Cups/Tablespoons/Teaspoons	Ounces	Grams/Milliliters
Butter	1 cup = 16 tablespoons = 2 sticks	8 ounces	230 grams
Cheese, shredded	1 cup	4 ounces	110 grams
Cream cheese	1 tablespoon	0.5 ounce	14.5 grams
Cornstarch	1 tablespoon	0.3 ounce	8 grams
Flour, all-purpose	1 cup/1 tablespoon	4.5 ounces/0.3 ounce	125 grams/8 grams
Flour, whole wheat	1 cup	4 ounces	120 grams
Fruit, dried	1 cup	4 ounces	120 grams
Fruits or veggies, chopped	1 cup	5 to 7 ounces	145 to 200 grams
Fruits or veggies, pureed	1 cup	8.5 ounces	245 grams
Honey, maple syrup, or corn syrup	1 tablespoon	0.75 ounce	20 grams
Liquids: cream, milk, water, or juice	1 cup	8 fluid ounces	240 milliliters
Oats	1 cup	5.5 ounces	150 grams
Salt	1 teaspoon	0.2 ounce	6 grams
Spices: cinnamon, cloves, ginger, or nutmeg (ground)	1 teaspoon	0.2 ounce	5 milliliters
Sugar, brown, firmly packed	1 cup	7 ounces	200 grams
Sugar, white	1 cup/1 tablespoon	7 ounces/0.5 ounce	200 grams/12.5 grams
Vanilla extract	1 teaspoon	0.2 ounce	4 grams

OVEN TEMPERATURES

Fahrenheit	Celsius	Gas Mark
225°	110°	¼
250°	120°	½
275°	140°	1
300°	150°	2
325°	160°	3
350°	180°	4
375°	190°	5
400°	200°	6
425°	220°	7
450°	230°	8

reference list

Alcott, Louisa M. *Little Women*. New York: Puffin Books, 2014.

Barrie, J. M., Anne McCaffrey, and F. D. Bedford. *Peter Pan*. New York: Modern Library, 2004.

Baum, L. Frank. *The Wonderful Wizard of Oz*. Luton, UK: Andrews UK Ltd, 2012.

Burnett, Frances H., and Margery Gill. *A Little Princess*. New York: Puffin Books, an imprint of Penguin Group USA, 2014.

Burnett, Frances H., and Tasha Tudor. *The Secret Garden*. New York: Harper & Row, 1987.

Carroll, Lewis. *Alice's Adventures in Wonderland and Through the Looking-Glass*. New York: Bantam Books, 1984.

Christie, Agatha. *Hickory, Dickory, Dock : A Hercule Poirot Mystery*. New York: Harper, 2011.

Christie, Agatha. *A Murder Is Announced*. New York: Dodd, Mead, 1985.

Christie, Agatha. *A Pocket Full of Rye*. New York: Dodd, Mead, 1981.

Dahl, Roald, and Quentin Blake. *James and the Giant Peach*. New York: Puffin Books, 2007.

Dickens, Charles. *A Christmas Carol*. New York: Bantam Books, 1986.

Doyle, Arthur Conan. *The Adventure of the Copper Beeches*. Trent, England: Solis Press, 2011.

Doyle, Arthur Conan. *The Five Orange Pips*. Maryland: Gunston LLC Trust, 2017.

Doyle, Arthur Conan. *The Naval Treaty*. City: Read Books Ltd., 2016.

Geoffrey of Monmouth. *The Life of Merlin, Vita Merlini*. United States: ReadaClassic.com, 2011.

Jacques, Brian. *The Legend of Luke*. New York: Ace Books, 2001.

Jacques, Brian, and Sean Rubin. *The Rogue Crew*. New York: Philomel Books, 2011.

Jacques, Brian, and David Elliot. *Triss*. New York: Philomel Books, 2002.

Leroux, Gaston, Mireille Ribiere, and Jann Matlock. *The Phantom of the Opera*. London: Penguin Books, 2012.

Lewis, C. S. *The Horse and His Boy*. New York: HarperCollins, 1994.

Lewis, C. S. *The Lion, the Witch, and the Wardrobe*. New York: HarperCollins, 1994.

Lewis, C. S. *The Magician's Nephew*. New York: HarperCollins, 1994.

London, Jack. *White Fang*. New York: Dover Publications, 1991.

Milne, A. A. *The House at Pooh Corner*. New York: Puffin Books, 1992.

Milne, A. A. *Winnie-the-Pooh*. New York: Dutton Children's Books, 1988.

Montgomery, L. M. *Anne of Avonlea: An Anne of Green Gables story*. New York: Grosset & Dunlap Publishers, 1990.

Montgomery, L. M. *Anne of Green Gables*. New York: Aladdin, 2014.

Norton, Mary. *The Borrowers*. New York: Harcourt, Brace & World, 1953.

Pyle, Howard. *The Story of King Arthur and His Knights*. New York: Barnes & Noble, 2012.

Shakespeare, William. *Romeo and Juliet*. New York: Modern Library Classics, 2009.

Stevenson, Robert L. *Treasure Island*. Richmond: Alma Classics, 2015.

Tolkien, J. R. R. *The Hobbit, or, There and Back Again*. Boston: Mariner Books, Houghton Mifflin Harcourt, 2012.

Twain, Mark. *The Adventures of Tom Sawyer*. New York: Barnes & Noble Classics, 2007.

index